MORAL AGENCY

within SOCIAL

STRUCTURES

and CULTURE

RELATED WORKS

Consumer Ethics in a Global Economy: How Buying Here Causes Injustice There
Daniel K. Finn

A World Free from Nuclear Weapons: The Vatican Conference on Disarmament
Drew Christiansen, SJ and Carole Sargent, Editors

The Vice of Luxury: Economic Excess in a Consumer Age
David Cloutier

Humanity in Crisis: Ethical and Religious Response to Refugees
David Hollenbach, SJ

A Culture of Engagement: Law, Religion, and Morality
Cathleen Kaveny

The Violence of Climate Change: Lessons of Resistance from Nonviolent Activists
Kevin J. O'Brien

Hope for Common Ground: Mediating the Personal and the Political in a Divided Church
Julie Hanlon Rubio

All God's Animals: A Catholic Theological Framework for Animal Ethics
Christopher Steck, SJ

MORAL AGENCY

within SOCIAL

STRUCTURES

and CULTURE

A PRIMER *on* CRITICAL REALISM *for* CHRISTIAN ETHICS

Edited by
DANIEL K. FINN

Foreword by MARGARET S. ARCHER | *Afterword by* LISA SOWLE CAHILL

Georgetown University Press / Washington, DC

The publisher is not responsible for third-party websites or their content. URL links were active at time of publication.

Library of Congress Cataloging-in-Publication Data

Names: Finn, Daniel K., 1947– editor.
Title: Moral Agency within Social Structures and Culture : A Primer on Critical Realism for Christian Ethics / [edited by] Daniel K. Finn.
Description: Washington, DC : Georgetown University Press, 2020. | Includes bibliographical references and index.
Identifiers: LCCN 2019035466 (print) | LCCN 2019035467 (ebook) | ISBN 9781626168008 (hardcover) | ISBN 9781626168015 (paperback) | ISBN 9781626168022 (ebook)
Subjects: LCSH: Christian ethics. | Social ethics. | Critical realism.
Classification: LCC BJ1251 .M627 2020 (print) | LCC BJ1251 (ebook) | DDC 241/.042—dc23
LC record available at https://lccn.loc.gov/2019035466
LC ebook record available at https://lccn.loc.gov/2019035467

20 19   9 8 7 6 5 4 3 2 First printing

Printed in the United States of America.
Cover design by Jeremy John Parker.

CONTENTS

FOREWORD

Margaret S. Archer

It takes humility, self-restraint, and courage to write a primer. Humility, because it puts the needs of others first and the authors' last; this is not the platform from which to trumpet one's own contributions and give a boost to one's latest publication. Self-restraint, because all the contributors know that they expose themselves to the cross-fire of competing interpretations with every intentionally simplified statement they venture, even within a single theoretical approach. Their knowledge of this danger generates a constant temptation to be self-protective by use of lengthy endnotes or defensive "scare" quotation marks. Courage, because almost every other theoretician will think they could have done a better job. This collection has all three virtues. In addition, it reveals that to write about ethics at any level is a normative task; ethical neutrality is a nonstarter, especially pedagogically, since what is presented is considered to be worthwhile.

Writing a primer about critical realism also requires Yiddish chutzpah, which, as Wikipedia puts it nicely, is "the quality of audacity, for good or for bad." Perhaps the only consensual response to critical realism is that it makes for tough reading, and its main contributors deserve no literary awards. There are exceptions, the best to my mind being Andrew Collier, Philip Gorski, Douglas Porpora, and Andrew Sayer for clarity without oversimplification. Hence the need, as in this primer, for audacious simplicity, for struggling with a concept, distilling it, and then conveying it without great loss. The contributors have generally adopted the good policy of being generous with illustrative examples that will remain lodged in readers' memories long after formal definitions have vaporized.

There is a final difficulty in introducing critical realism. Roy Bhaskar, the founding philosophical force in critical realism, wrote his books in what we colloquially call stages of his intellectual journey: (1) realism and science, (2) realism in the social sciences, (3) the dialectic, and (4) metareality. We avowed critical realists often accentuate only one of these. For example, many of us leading theorists, especially if our competence and interests are vested in the social sciences, will call ourselves "stage 2" critical realists, which goes for most of those named so far, because we can relate most readily to it and make most of it in relation to our existing competence.

I would call the present volume a "stage 2 book," putting critical realist sociology to work illuminating the character of moral agency in social life. There is nothing pejorative in saying so. We are usually powerfully drawn to those aspects of social theory that seem most useful to us.

There is one last introductory comment that it seems important to make. This concerns how Bhaskar saw his contribution in relation to other disciplines. As an Oxford philosopher, he defined his role without hubris as being an "under-laborer" for the social sciences. What he was undertaking was a philosophical ground-clearing task; how we in social science would afterward till the soil and what we would produce from it was up to us. We in sociology have employed these basic philosophical convictions to develop an improved understanding of structure and culture. They have a powerful influence on people. They exercise their causal powers through the (altered) decisions that people make. But how? An answer is just as pressing in this primer as in any other research. I have argued for "reflexivity" as the missing mediatory mechanism, and some of the collaborators in this volume have taken this up, as has Christian Smith.[1] All of these considerations lead us to ask two questions: What has Bhaskar's "under-labouring" done for social theorizing, and why is it of relevance to Christian ethics?

It is sometimes noted that the approach to which any given social theory is most intransigently opposed affects it more deeply than anything else. This is true of critical realism and is distinctive of most of its adherents; we are like terriers, continually shaking the rat we have killed for fear of its resuscitation. This rat's name is empiricism. In David Hume's formulation—the most influential for social sciences—it does indeed show remarkable powers of recovery. Today the hype surrounding the digital access to "big data" supplies empiricism with a new life-support system. If that data is universal for a population, even in the case of Facebook that vaunts near-global coverage, what more can a social scientist want? To the critical realist, some of the most significant elements get left out. And this concern is distinct from valid methodological criticisms about data quality.

Fundamentally, David Hume declared war upon causality (see chapter 3). He denied all the "how" questions and insisted that, at best, we should content ourselves with the manifest associations revealed between parts of any data set. The goal was limited to establishing constant conjunctions between observable variables, that is, ones that depended exclusively on sense data, and their invariable succession or sequence. In other words, "A" and "B" correlated or co-varied like children's height and weight, but without any ability to say why. Thus, elementary questions such as "Did A cause B?" or "Did B cause A?" or "Did both result from C?" were beyond empiricism's explanatory bounds. Today this results in national reports blandly and vacuously asserting that, for instance, "migration results from poverty" simply because they are correlated. Even nineteenth-century census statistics effectively queried such facile statements. During the Irish potato famines of the 1840s, in every county affected, one person remained for each person who migrated, and this was often the case within the same family. Thus, "poverty" had no uniform impact on emigration. Rather, it produced a variety of responses whose differences beg for explanation.

It presents a causal puzzle. One or more factors beyond the blighted stores of potatoes must have been involved, and the puzzle is not solved by invoking folk psychology that it was the most adventurous who migrated, or the unmarried, or any other variable that could be added to, extracted from, or induced on the basis of the data mix available. Such reactions are what fuelled more and more elaborate social statistics, such as the sophisticated mathematical models now dominant in main-stream economics. However, playing with patterns does not eliminate causality; it results only in a hydraulic account in terms of pushes and pulls in which the human actor is merely the billiard ball who is at their mercy.

In his first book, A Realist Theory of Science, Bhaskar articulated the notion of "causal powers" operative in the natural world.[2] These were not matters simply of collection, inspection, or detecting patterns, as these all deal with observable phenomena—the sense-perceptible. These practices worked for natural scientists because the scientists themselves constructed a sterile laboratory, closed against dis-torting intrusions from the real world.

The lesson for social scientists is that this route is closed to them. Society is intrinsically an open system in which the powers of its components interacted, sus-pended, or accentuated one another. There is nothing mystical about such powers that are not sense-perceptible. They are ontologically real and have real causal impact, even though empiricists cannot speak of them because of an epistemologi-cal choice to limit their attention to the sense-perceptible effects of these powers. Imagine a small boat chugging along a river powered by its outboard motor. If its propeller encounters weeds that twine around it, the boat stops. But unless it is damaged, the motor retains its causal power to drive the boat forward if the strands of weeds are severed and detached. Further, consider some of the array of real causal powers displayed in this simple example: a belief in a causal mechanism and disbelief in voodoo, someone capable of swimming, the availability of a sturdy knife, a propeller strong enough for its blades not to have sheared off, the patience of those on board, no hazard posed by other traffic on the river, and so on. This is no laboratory but part of ordinary life in an open system, and it is about that we must all theorize, though we do this fallibly, whether we are social scientists or ordinary folk.

So what is the role of the realist ontology in sociology? To understand the various parts of the social world, every social theory is founded on ontological assumptions of one kind or another. Critical realist sociologists strive to make their ontology explicit, but in many other frameworks analogous assumptions remain implicit and often unexamined.

In itself a realist social ontology explains *nothing*, but importantly it excludes vari-ous inadequate explanations. Examples of the latter include social constructionism (because it exchanges epistemology for ontology), holism (because causal powers are not deterministic social forces), and methodological individualism (because it views the social order as an aggregate of individual acts). As such, the realist social ontology plays a regulative role; it eliminates some social concepts as inadmissible in description or explanation (just as atheism eliminates divine providence as the cause of anything). A social ontology clears the ground but tells no one how to explain anything. For this task, an explanatory programme is required, cast in terms of the causal powers of those entities involved in shaping a specific social context with its own emergent powers at a higher level (see chapter 2 for critical realism's stratified social ontology).

So far the explanatory programme—its place, work, and limits—has been poorly understood. My own approach to how distributions of socially scarce resources, roles, organizations, and social institutions came to be structured in a particular way and to exert the powers that they do has often been called a theory. In fact, it has more affinity with methodology, one that helps the investigator to break up the complex flow of events and actual occurrences over time into three temporal phases that make a specific research problem tractable.

Time is essential, whether of short duration (boy meets girl in the university coffee bar, and they become a couple) or a much longer period (for the development of an education system in a nation). In short, there is no such thing as "decontextualized action"; we never just *find* ourselves in a situation. The context is always already shaped by prior interactions. As Auguste Comte rightly maintained, the majority of actors are the dead. How did that boy and girl come to enter that particular university (unlike their poorer friends), and why does it have the character and location it has? How did the emperor Napoleon attain the nearly complete freedom to redesign the educational system of France without ceding much to the Catholic Church that had built and staffed existing schools?

The causal powers of structure (and culture) work diachronically over tracts of time different from those of personal agency because structure (and culture) necessarily predate the actions that reproduce or transform them and because structural (and cultural) change necessarily postdate those actions. This is what makes this explanatory programme a matter of analytical dualism and not philosophical dualism. Thus, after their first encounter, subsequent interaction between the two students has to occur beyond drinking that one cup of coffee together; they must do something regularly before becoming "an item." Only if these and other doings prove mutually agreeable and they meet with little opposition are they on their way to marriage. All the explanatory programme has done is to break up the flow of a myriad of tiny episodes, seemingly lacking in significance. This is similar to the fundamental sequence of social change by which a given social form or state is altered by its ineradicable dependence on the actions of persons: the context is structurally conditioned, decisions are taken and actions undertaken in that context, and social structural elaboration takes place in the third phase—either sustaining or transforming the structural context.

Historic structuring that shaped institutions in a particular way and validated their practices goes a long way toward accounting for the impact of actions to either support or challenge that context. The interactions of vested interests of past winners, the antagonism of past losers, and the motivation of different groups eventuate in stability or change.

Nevertheless, if the explanatory programme passes muster, once again it explains *nothing*. It is only the investigator who does, in advancing what I have called a "practical social theory," namely, one that accounts for the phenomenon in question, be it a particular marriage or a specific educational system. Yet the question remains: What makes for a satisfactory explanation by a satisfactory theory? Can critical realism help us any further here?

I think that, indeed, it can, and various chapters of this book (chapters 4, 5, 6, and 7) illustrate how. Structure, culture, and agency are different kinds of emergent entities with different properties and causal powers, despite the fact that they are crucial for one another's formation, continuation, or transformation. Critical realism insists not only on "activity dependence" (actions shape context) but also on "contextual dependence" (structure influences agency and culture) and "concept dependence" (culture influences agency and structure). All three are simultaneously indispensable to any concrete explanation because agents not only have to do things (taking particular courses of action, in circumstances not of their own making) but also need some understanding of why they entertain the aspirations that motivate their actions.

In the critical realist search for "generative mechanisms," only some mixture of these three components—structure, culture, and agency—can account for specific forms of stability and change in the social order. Thus, to explain, for example, the success of any subgroup pursuing ethical ends within any larger faith grouping depends on not only giving each of the three elements its due but also acknowledging that the emergent relations among the three are complementary or contradictory, which is a second-order property reflecting critical realism's stratified social ontology.

Since the 1950s in developed countries, Christian ethics have suffered a bumpy downhill trajectory. I speak here of Christian ethics primarily as ethics lived out in the world, not as the academic discipline with that name. This presents an immense challenge to the present volume in which there is insufficient space for their detailed examination. First, there was an almost exclusive preoccupation with the "secularization question." Put as a simple question, was declining church attendance indicative of the decline of "religion" both as an institution in society and as a moral guide to the populace?

Second, defence of the enduring relevance of Christian ethics resorted to such formulas as "implicit religion" or "believing without belonging." Effectively, these conceded the marginalization of religious institutions but defended the moral relevance of Christian teaching as a guide to action, individual or collective. In short, religion had become privatized and was increasingly excluded from the public sphere (except on certain ceremonial occasions).

Third, the growth of multiculturalism in the West, with arrivals from each country or area mistakenly being treated as homogeneous, fostered inclusion as the top priority, ignoring intragroup ethical differences in order to further social integration. For example, Prince Charles's desire to be crowned as "Defender of the Faiths" (plural) seems to imply—morally and questionably—that to have faith in something is preferable to having none in anything. This is not a defence of free speech, since it ignores ethical contradictions between faiths, which some governments could not tolerate (French constitutional *laicité*) and which some social movements morally abominate (such as the restrictions placed upon women in many faith groupings).

Fourth, on this downward slope was the crucial "macro-moral disconnect," as Douglas Porpora terms it, where the privatization of religion resulted in its moral attrition. This is neatly summarized in the titles of two of his books: *Landscapes of the Soul: The Loss of Moral Meaning in American Life* and *Post-Ethical Society*.[3] His argument is complemented by my own analysis of the loss of moral reference that had previously been held to ground the legitimacy of law (such as Hans Kelsen's *grundnorm*) and the increasing reliance of public and private authorities upon mere regulations whose efficacy was without normative underpinning but relied upon penalty alone (fines, temporary bans, exclusions). These encouraged the population to behave as *homo economicus*, asking calculatedly about, say, a parking fine: "Is paying a fine worth it to me?" rather than "Is it wrong to park illegally?"[4]

Fifth, we are now confronting the "post-truth" society. Truth itself is a value, even though we know that our efforts to describe any state of affairs will always be fallible. However, to believe that that ideological conviction, rather than the actual state of affairs being described, is the appropriate standard of judgment of those efforts will inevitably undermine most social institutions. Ecological policies built upon climate change denial (chapter 6) are a good illustration, but so too are the politics of manipulation, economics built on false forecasts, medicine and health care at the mercy of arbitrary drug pricing, and, above all, human relations based upon duplicity.

This crude delineation of the five phases is an attempt to highlight the fate of Christian morality over the last six decades in the developed world. It is obviously fallible because it is susceptible to discovering overlap between phases and countervailing mechanisms at work throughout. It is only introduced at the end to pose a question about this primer. By sticking to stage 2 of critical realism, is it possible to give an adequate account of the shifting role of Christian ethics in public and private life over the past sixty years?

Of course, the aim of this volume is to employ critical realism not just for better descriptions but to employ those better descriptions for an improved moral analysis. Personally, I think that readers and researchers in ethics will welcome this volume and will, I hope, begin to employ the resources of critical realism in their own work.

NOTES

1. Christian Smith, *What Is a Person? Rethinking Humanity, Social Life, and the Moral Good from the Person Up* (Chicago: University of Chicago Press, 2010), 61–65.
2. Roy Bhaskar, *A Realist Theory of Science* (New York: Verso, 1975).
3. Douglas V. Porpora, *Landscapes of the Soul: The Loss of Moral Meaning in American Life* (New York: Oxford University Press, 2001); and Douglas V. Porpora, Alexander Nikolaev, Julia Hagemann May, Alexander Jenkins, *Post-Ethical Society: The Iraq War, Abu Ghraib, and the Moral Failure of the Secular* (Chicago: University of Chicago Press, 2013).
4. Margaret S. Archer, "Anormative Social Regulation: The Attempt to Cope with Social Morphogenesis," in *Morphogenesis and the Crisis of Normativity*, ed. Margaret S. Archer, 141–68 (Cham, Switzerland: Springer, 2015).

CHAPTER 1

How Critical Realism Can Help Christian Social Ethics

David Cloutier

Christian social ethics is about Christian ethics and about society. From its beginnings, Christianity wrestled theologically with questions of the social order and engaged in controversy over the actions of civil authorities. But the present configuration of "Christian social ethics" emerges in the late nineteenth century, in both Protestantism and Catholicism. Within the academy, new spaces for completely secular "social sciences" were increasingly powerful, and within society, science-inspired movements like social Darwinism and Marxism shaped social practice. How should Christian ethics interact with these new configurations of knowledge about society? Multiple influences have given birth to a wide variety of approaches. The aim of this volume is to indicate how a particularly insightful form of social science—critical realist sociology—can improve each of these.

VARIETIES OF DISCOURSE

Helping to sort out the variety of approaches, James Gustafson, in his work for the World Council of Churches, developed a typology of four sorts of discourse evident within social ethics.[1] The first is "prophetic discourse," whose primary purposes run parallel to those of Israel's prophets: to offer sweeping indictments of the current situation, to kindle hope for a "more utopian form" of society, and to evoke "a sense of urgency."[2] A second form Gustafson calls "narrative discourse." Its primary role is to "sustain the identity of the community through memory" but in its "parabolic" form can also offer specific stories that "suggest courses of action in particular circumstances."[3]

1

The third form he labeled "ethical," and it is "rationally rigorous" in making "precise distinctions" and using "syllogistic logic."[4] This sort of discourse is valuable because it shapes with greater rigor the identification of middle axioms and proximate principles that name what we ought to do. The fourth form of discourse he identifies as "policy," which is not so much what we *ought* to do as what it is *possible* for us to do right here and now. It "seeks to determine what is desirable within the constraints of what is possible."[5] The third and fourth forms are related, but whereas the third form relies on a historical tradition of philosophical inquiry worked out with some precision, the fourth form is much more attentive to particular circumstances and dynamics.

While appreciative of these forms of social ethical discourse, Gustafson identifies shortcomings of each. He is concerned that prophecy and narrative lack a self-consciousness about their limitations. Prophetic discourse "dramatizes," he says, but "cannot inform incremental choices" when "good and bad are comingled," especially since it stresses an "ideal future" at the expense of short-range possibilities.[6] Narrative discourse is limited in its ability to speak to "those who do not share its authority" and requires "more rationally rigorous" means to do the inevitable task of choosing an order of priority among the multitude of possible stories and symbols one can find in the Christian tradition.[7]

Gustafson sees a shortcoming in ethical and policy approaches as well. He implies that a Christian social ethics merely of precise philosophical distinctions and wonky applications would not only be uninspiring but more importantly would be incomplete in its overall worldview. For example, it would be problematic to suggest the term "justice" would receive its form only through the working out of the philosophical tradition without biblical influences. Moreover, Gustafson also worries that policy discussions and conclusions can seem indistinguishable from what one might find in more popular, secular journals of opinion.

ENTER CRITICAL REALISM

The aim of this chapter is not to evaluate Gustafson's typology or his own views on the four forms of social ethical discourse. Nor is it to provide a new analysis of the four or to call for an integration or balancing of the various forms of discourse. The point is to argue that critical realism—a metaethical perspective on the natural and social worlds—can improve each of the four approaches in ways that scholars employing that approach would value. This is done by providing each a more precise and insightful understanding of how social structures and culture, on the one hand, arise from and depend on the moral agency of individual persons but, on the other, simultaneously exert a causal influence on those persons by altering their actions and in the long run shaping the character of each. This chapter is not the place to explain critical realism in detail, but we can start by naming a few key insights that distinguish a critical realist approach, indicating their worth in enhancing each of the different types of social ethics.

As Daniel Finn explains in more detail in chapters 3 and 4, critical realism offers a metatheory for explaining both the real causal force of social structure on human agents and the impact of agents on structures. This social scientific analysis grows out of the philosophy of science and, for the purposes of this chapter, can be understood to resist two sorts of reductionist explanations for human action. The first reduces structures to individual free choices. This sort of "methodological individualism" assumes an unconditioned—more precisely, an unpositioned—individual as the agent exercising free choice. Critical realism recognizes how individuals take on a variety of positions in social structures throughout the day and how their choices to attain their goals (whatever they may be) are altered by the restrictions and opportunities they face within those structures. On the other hand, the second sort of reductionism explains (away) individual moral agency in the face of powerful social forces—often characterized as "laws" but sometimes as a broader, more complex entity called "culture." Critical realism recognizes that the power of culture and structure is actuated only through the free-but-constrained decisions made by acting persons.

These two reductionisms create what Christian Smith characterizes as "a Homo duplex model of humanity" that "assumes that two basic realities exist—individuals and society—and that between them a primal opposition and divergence of interests operates."[8] Each of these flawed explanatory models then prioritizes one over the other. To correct for this, ethicists sometimes attempt a "both/and" balance between them, but unfortunately this is typically done without attending to the fundamental reductionism that creates the duplex model in the first place.

Critical realism aims to avoid both forms of reductionism by emphasizing that human agents are always positioned within already existing social structures that possess real causal force. Yet structures and cultures have causal impact only through their influence on the decisions of agents. Agents are always positioned and constrained, but they really do exercise their own powers too. Neither agents nor structures exist independently of one another, but there is no inherent conflict in which the explanation of one must be reduced to the other. Both are real, but differently so. An analogous set of insights are available concerning the relation of culture and individual choice, as Matthew Shadle explains in chapter 5. Resisting a "myth of cultural integration" that views culture as a totalizing whole, critical realism insists that any "cultural system" includes a variety of (sometimes conflicting) resources that precede (and therefore shape) agents but that agents are also creative users of these resources in their interactions.

This recognition of the problems of reductionism should be particularly attractive for Christian social ethicists, given the anthropological assumptions that are widely shared within the field. The freedom of agents is a necessary condition of any account of moral responsibility, yet the Christian tradition also believes agents are inherently, and not merely accidentally, social. Being social is constitutive of what it means to be a human person. Amid modern tendencies toward one reductionism or the other, Christian social ethics is best served by a social theory that can make sense of the relationship of these two claims adequately, providing a social scientific view that comports well with a theological understanding of human freedom. Critical realism certainly does so.

Because it does, even this very brief sketch of the approach can help us see how it might enhance the four types of discourse identified by Gustafson. The first two types—the prophetic and the narrative—have become more prominent precisely because Christians have become more self-consciously aware of the importance of broader, structural questions for social ethics. In particular, there is a much more vivid awareness of how the scriptural texts themselves address larger social structures, often in very challenging ways. Readings of the New Testament that depict an essentially non-Jewish Jesus offering quietistic moral advice to individuals have been recognized by both perspectives as historically irresponsible.

Yet, as Gustafson intimates, these discourses often face challenges. While the texts do frequently name particular moral responsibilities—for example, the prophets explicitly call for acts of repentance and sustenance for the poor—they do so in imprecise ways, and indeed their particular suggestions sometimes appear to cut in different directions. One needs a social analysis to connect scriptural images and ideas to particular responsibilities in contemporary situations. Yet too often this analysis is a totalizing materialist or cultural critique, unwittingly participating in what Margaret Archer calls "the myth of cultural integration."[9] That is, scriptural images are tied to overly sweeping analyses of the realities of modern societies. At their most extreme, as I have argued in detail elsewhere, prophetic or narrative critiques of this sort can lead to paralysis or to entirely either-or rejections of existing conditions.[10] Critical realism can be helpful here because, while it takes the causal power of structures seriously, it avoids a totalizing reductionism or (even worse) a reification that renders agential responsibility moot. Instead, critical realism can enhance the authentic task of prophetic and narrative modes: to describe in vivid, moral terms the directions and forces existing in any given time and place, and to provide forceful, imaginative reasons for agents to pursue ends that structures might otherwise make difficult and unattractive or that existing cultural configurations of ideas might impede. What critical realism can do is provide a clearer place for prophecy and narrative to do their ethical work.

Critical realism also supplements the third type of social ethical discourse. A preoccupation with precision of definition can sometimes become an end in itself. If we accept Alasdair MacIntyre's claims, we should recognize that moral concepts always have a history—indeed, a socially embodied history—and so cannot function as ahistorical foundational assertions from which we directly deduce further principles or applications.[11] For some, this recognition of "historical consciousness" in ethics can lead to a kind of cultural relativism that ultimately dissolves the task of ethics. However, for others, the greater temptation is to believe that the task is just to "get the definitions right" and then deduce moral responsibilities from these. Critical realism enables us to avoid both a facile relativism or a static, "classicist" deductionism. Instead, these moral concepts should be used carefully in the analysis of both structure and culture in any given society, impinging on the choices made by the reflective, enstructured agent. Daniel Daly's chapter on critical realism's contribution to virtue ethics particularly shows how this works (see chapter 8).[12]

Finally, the relevance of a critical realist approach for enhancing policy discourse should be obvious. By providing a better understanding of the relation of structure and agency, it illuminates the places where agents can or should act to transform structures. Indeed, combining the moral convictions of Christian social ethics with the insights offered by critical realism would make for more persuasive policy analysis than any alternative, even in the broader public sphere.

AN EXAMPLE

Matthew Shadle's chapter 7 looks in more detail at how crucial realism illuminates economic life, but here we might simply consider the ways that critical realism's more detailed description of social structures proves useful in the long-standing debate about Christianity's relation to capitalism. Central to Catholic social thought on the issue is the encyclical *Centesimus annus*, by St. John Paul II. The discussion of this document often becomes a pro-versus-anti oversimplification, with scholars on the Right and Left appealing to different statements within the document.

What is sometimes overlooked is that, in the encyclical, John Paul gave an account of a morally good "business economy": "an economic system which recognizes the fundamental and positive role of business, the market, private property and the resulting responsibility for the means of production, as well as free human creativity in the economic sector." Yet "freedom in the economic sector" must be "circumscribed within a strong juridical framework which places it at the service of human freedom in its totality, and which sees it as a particular aspect of that freedom, the core of which is ethical and religious."[13]

According to the principle of the universal destination of goods, ownership entails responsibility. Some of that responsibility is for the common good, and so ownership is reasonably subject to laws made by legitimate governments for the sake of the common good. Employing a critical realist lens, we can see that the pope is speaking of agents (who do right or wrong) and structures (which necessarily shape the agents, sometimes in sinful ways). Rather than arguing over broad visions, the question for social ethicists seeking to apply John Paul's description in any given nation should be, What about *our* agents? What about *our* structures? These questions don't have to entail purely oppositional understandings: capitalism versus socialism, business versus labor, the rich versus the poor (though all these tensions are present within any given structural reality). Instead, they are questions about specifying the responsibilities of agents within structures (and culture) set up and aimed in a certain way.

Any answer is, as the pope says, "obviously complex." Thus, social ethics should work diligently to name and sort out the complexities, and critical realism is immensely helpful in doing this. Take one aspect of John Paul's description: understanding a business as "a community of persons" who seek to "satisfy their basic needs" by forming "a particular group at the service of the whole of society."[14] Therefore, businesses are to understand themselves in relation to the society in a particular way. This is evidently a normative description, and critical realism cannot (and does not aspire to) offer an alternative normative answer. Rather, it gives us the tools to make sense of the agents and structures that already exist as well as a template on which we can reimagine those relationships in a way that accords with the pope's normative description, which calls us to consider the position of "businessperson" that agents enter into in our society.

This social position comes with a set of relations to other social positions: supervisor, subordinates, stockholders (or an owner), other businesses, customers, professional organizations, government offices, and so on. Critical realism provides a helpful way to describe these interactions. Social structures entail a system of relations among preexisting social positions. Because of this, upon entering into this position, this particular person faces objectively given restrictions, enablements, and incentives generated by the social structure. Critical realist sociologist Margaret Archer speaks of the vested interests, opportunity costs, and situational logics exerting causal influence in each such situation. These analytical tools can make more precise any discussion of the character of economic life.

A similar sort of analysis could be used to give a better, richer account of operationalizing "the preferential option for the poor," especially in a way that reflects this principle structurally, and not just as a too-vague sentiment. No one doubts the fundamental Christian imperative to assist the poor (at least they shouldn't). Nevertheless, the question of how to specify that responsibility for agents and for structures is hard. Practicing the prophetic call would benefit from a better account of the structural and cultural configurations within which the poor are disadvantaged as well as more effective ways to account for the personal agency of both the rich and the poor.

CONCLUSION

The aim here in this introductory chapter is not to work out the details of an ethical analysis of economic life employing these insights from sociology but simply to point to the potential contributions that critical realism can make in improving the analytic capacity of social ethics. And while the example above is from one particular tradition, critical realism would be helpful to all Christian social ethicists speaking in any of the different registers and modes Gustafson identifies. In the following chapter, Theodora Hawksley presents a more general evaluation of the shortcomings on Catholic social teaching's understanding of social embodiments of evil, finding there too that a crucial realist perspective helps to avoid an individualistic analysis.

The rest of this primer aims at throwing more light on these claims in two ways. First, in chapters 3, 4, and 5, Daniel Finn and Matthew Shadle provide a more detailed analysis of what critical realism is, including its view of the natural world and its resulting sociological analysis of social structures and culture. The subsequent chapters in the collection then begin the task of showing how a critical realist approach can be used to deepen Christian ethical reflection on specific topics. Particular attention is paid to topics that feature large and vexing structural questions. Chapter 6, by David Cloutier, addresses the ecological crisis, while chapter 7, by Matthew Shadle, applies the insights of crucial realism to economic life. Chapter 8, by Daniel Daly, asks how critical realism can improve our understanding of virtue, both its exercise and its cultivation. A final section provides the reader with suggestions for further reading.

We, the authors of this volume, believe that the analysis of structure and culture provided by critical realist sociology can be deeply helpful throughout Christian theology. It can improve the way ecclesiology understands the internal dynamics of a church, the way patristics explains the influence of Roman authorities on the Fathers, the way liturgical theology understands the formative dimension of weekly worship, the way biblical studies interpret the mutual influences of different literary traditions, the way fundamental moral theology explains the influence of society on the virtue of individuals, the way pastoral theology describes the relation between pastor and lay ministers, the way bioethicists understand the relation of doctor and patient in a health crisis, and more. For simplicity, and given the backgrounds of the authors, this book focuses on how critical realism can help Christian social ethics.

The primary literature in critical realism—both in the philosophy of science and sociology—can be daunting. This primer is not meant to provide definitive treatments of either critical realism or the topics in question. Instead, it is intended as a basic introduction that offers just enough of a taste of the advantages of critical realism to invite other scholars to make these tools their own by turning afterward to the original sources. If we can persuade you, the reader, to do that, this book will be a success.

NOTES

1. James Gustafson, "An Analysis of Church and Society Social Ethical Writings," *Ecumenical Review* 40 (1988): 267–78.
2. Gustafson, 269–70.
3. Gustafson, 272.
4. Gustafson, 269.
5. Gustafson, 270.

6. Gustafson, 269.

7. Gustafson.

8. Christian Smith, *To Flourish or Destruct: A Personalist Theory of Human Goods, Motivations, Failure, and Evil* (Chicago: University of Chicago Press, 2015), 56.

9. Margaret Archer, "The Myth of Cultural Integration," *British Journal of Sociology* 36 (1985): 333–53.

10. David Cloutier, "Cavanaugh and Grimes on Structural Evils of Violence and Race: Overcoming Conflicts in Contemporary Social Ethics," *Journal of the Society of Christian Ethics* 37, no. 2 (Fall 2017): 59–78.

11. This is the core claim of the first eight chapters of MacIntyre's *After Virtue: A Study in Moral Theory* (Notre Dame, IN: University of Notre Dame Press, 1981), and still grounds MacIntyre's insistence, in his latest book, that moral agents must achieve "a kind of sociological self-knowledge" for successful practical reason. See Alasdair MacIntyre, *Ethics in the Conflicts of Modernity: An Essay on Desire, Practical Reasoning, and Narrative* (Cambridge: Cambridge University Press, 2016), 112.

12. Ultimately, such an approach should take with full seriousness—and more precision—MacIntyre's understanding of moral agency as about virtues that are always embedded in configurations of social practices, as best explained in his *Whose Justice? Which Rationality?* (Notre Dame, IN: University of Notre Dame Press, 1988). That is, moral notions or concepts function first and foremost as virtues of agents, but agents who must engage in socially constituted practices and construe reasons for acting on various desires as "good" or not.

13. John Paul II, Encyclical Letter *Centesimus annus*, May 1, 1991, 42.

14. John Paul II, 35.

CHAPTER 2

How Critical Realism Can Help Catholic Social Teaching

Theodora Hawksley

In chapter 1, David Cloutier argues that critical realism can enrich any of the four forms of social ethical discourse identified by James Gustafson in Christian social ethics, both Protestant and Catholic. This chapter looks more particularly at Catholic social teaching to argue that post–Vatican II developments to address social evil, while helpful, need further resources to accomplish the task and that the work of critical realist Roy Bhaskar is a rich source for that assistance.

This chapter briefly surveys the development of language about social sin in the Catholic social teaching tradition and finds that this leaves us with a further question: Is that language adequate? The answer is, "Partly, yes, but something more is needed." The situation at present is rather like a selection test for army officers, where would-be recruits, working together, have to arrange an assortment of ropes, barrels, and planks in order to climb from point A to point B without touching the ground. The "point B" that Catholic social teaching must reach is clear: we need an understanding of the ways in which moral evil takes social shape, one that enables us to name it and respond to it effectively. Catholic theologians are thus faced with the task of rearranging and adapting the existing resources of the tradition—our conceptual equivalents of barrels and planks—in order to get there.

Although a simple rearrangement of the tradition gets us some way toward our goal, it falls short: it does not provide us with an adequate account of how moral evil takes social shape. Part of the issue here is with the materials, in that the basic concepts of Catholic moral theology that we are using to get from A to B cannot in fact get us there. We need to borrow something, and that "something more," the authors of this volume argue, is critical realism: it gives us one way of bridging the gap to an account of the social dimension of moral evil. It is perhaps not the only way to bridge the gap and perhaps not a perfect way, but our claim in this book is that critical realism basically works: it does the work of satisfactorily describing how moral evil takes social shape in a way that also helps us to respond to it.

The purpose of this chapter is to give brief answers to the question just raised, surveying what the existing Catholic social teaching tradition has to say about the social dimension of moral evil and pointing out the ways in which that language falls short. The way is then clear for the rest of the book to set out the "something more" that critical realism can offer to Catholic social teaching and moral theology.

PRECONCILIAR MORAL THEOLOGY

In order to understand some of the constraints on the language of social sin as it develops in the period following the Second Vatican Council, it will be helpful to give a sketch of the characteristics and concerns of preconciliar moral theology. In what John O'Malley calls the "long nineteenth century," Catholic moral theology came to be dominated by the manualist tradition.[1] The Council of Trent had decreed that laypeople were to confess their sins once a year, specifying which mortal sins they had committed and how often. The manualist tradition therefore developed as a way of training priests to hear confessions, to make sure their penitents confessed their sins well. This meant training priests to identify exactly what sin had been committed and to assign the appropriate penance. The result was the emergence of a kind of moral theology that was very sin-focused, very individual-focused, and very act-focused. Over time, it led to what John A. Mahoney describes as

> an approach to the moral life as discontinuous; "freezing" the film in a jerky succession of individual "stills" to be analysed, and ignoring the plot. Continuity was discounted, or at most only a "circumstance," and the "story" of the individual's moral vocation and exploration either unsuspected or disregarded.[2]

Because preconciliar theology was geared toward accurately establishing what sinful acts a particular person had done, it meant that the social dimensions of the moral life were occluded. The influence of relationships and social structures on a person's action, for good or ill, was not really in view. It also meant that whole categories of sinful action were largely lost to view. In the immediately preconciliar period, the Church was preoccupied with antimodernism and was focused on issues of internal Church order. James Keenan, surveying a selection of moral manuals from the period, bluntly observes, "One only has to see that girls' dresses and sperm receive more attention than atomic weapons to appreciate how distant the manualists were from the world as it emerged out of the rubble of the Second World War and faced the possibility of nuclear war."[3]

SOCIAL SIN

It is against this background that the language of social sin emerges in the period following the Second Vatican Council. The documents of Vatican II themselves do not use the explicit language of social sin. The phrase *"peccatum sociale"* appeared in a draft of a conciliar document, but objections from the floor that the idea of "social sin" undermined personal responsibility were heeded, and the final document spoke only of the "social consequences of sin."[4] Nevertheless, in some sections of *Gaudium et spes* there is a move toward moral analysis of social structures and an acknowledgment that social structures can shape moral agents in adverse ways. *Gaudium et spes* speaks of "institutions, laws and modes of thinking and feeling . . . handed down from previous generations," stating,

> When the structure of affairs is flawed by the consequences of sin, man, already born with a bent toward evil, finds there new inducements to sin, which cannot be overcome without strenuous efforts and the assistance of grace.[5]

The document also moves toward a more contextual and dynamic understanding of the human person, admitting that people "are often diverted from doing good and spurred towards evil by the social circumstances in which they live and are immersed from their birth."[6]

The Episcopal Conference of Latin America, in its meetings at Medellín, Colombia (1968), and Puebla, Mexico (1979), take this language further. Confronting the situations of poverty and political repressions in their countries, the bishops talk about serious sins "reflected in" unjust structures and "sinful situations" (Medellín), sinful economic systems, and the "sinful structures" of people's personal and social lives (Puebla).[7] Although often careful to include "individual" in the same breath as "social," these documents use the language of social sin, sinful institutions, and sinful structures confidently and without justification.

In his closing address at Puebla, John Paul II stated that one can speak only of "social" or "structural" sin in an analogical sense, and from this point on, magisterial notes of caution are sounded more frequently.[8] John Paul II's apostolic exhortation *Reconciliatio et paenitentia* (1984) manifests a desire to engage with language of social sin but also warns of the danger of undermining the significance of personal sin. The section on personal and social sin begins with a caution:

> Sin, in the proper sense, is always a personal act, since it is an act of freedom on the part of an individual and not properly of a group or community. This individual may be conditioned, incited and influenced by numerous and powerful external factors. He may also be subjected to tendencies, defects and habits linked with his personal condition. In not a few cases such external and internal factors may attenuate, to a greater or lesser degree, the person's freedom and therefore his responsibility and guilt. But it is a truth of faith, also

confirmed by our experience and reason, that the human person is free. This truth cannot be disregarded in order to place the blame for individuals' sins on external factors such as structures, systems or other people. Above all, this would be to deny the person's dignity and freedom which are manifested— even though in a negative and disastrous way—also in this responsibility for sin committed.[9]

The document then goes on to discuss three permissible meanings of the term "social sin" and one inadmissible meaning. Social sin can refer, first of all, to the way in which every individual's sin affects others: there is a "communion of sin" as well as a "communion of saints."[10] Second, social sin can also mean any act or omission that harms our neighbour, including sins against justice.[11] Third, coming closer to Medellín and Puebla, John Paul II also says that social sin can mean "relationships between the various human communities . . . not always in accordance with the plan of God," and he names the class struggle and "obstinate opposition" between blocs of nations—although he describes these as "social evils" rather than social sin. He goes on to ask

> whether moral responsibility for these evils, and therefore sin, can be attributed to any person in particular . . . realities and situations such as those described, when they become generalized and reach vast proportions as social phenomena, almost always become anonymous, just as their causes are complex and not always identifiable. Hence if once speaks of social sin here, the expression obviously has an analogical meaning.[12]

He then reaffirms that any definition of social sin that contrasts it with personal sin in order to dodge the latter and lodge blame with "some vague entity or anonymous collectivity such as the situation, the system, society, structures, or institutions" is inadmissible.[13] Rather,

> whenever the church speaks of situations of sin or when she condemns as social sins certain situations or the collective behavior of certain groups . . . she knows and proclaims that such cases of social sin are the result of the accumulation and concentration of many personal sins. . . . The real responsibility, then, lies with individuals.[14]

John Paul II is clearly prepared to go beyond the Council Fathers, for whom any language of "social sin" undermined personal responsibility, but his careful circumscription of the precise meanings that social sin can and cannot have demonstrates that the same worry persists. The first two permissible senses of social sin might be more accurately characterized by the phrase used in *Sacrosanctum concilium*, the "social consequences of sin": social sin here means that our (individual) sins have effects on others and that we (as individuals) can sin against social relationships. His third sense of social sin comes closer, but here it seems that the idea of sin as a conscious act of individual wrongdoing has just been scaled up; in referring to the class struggle and ideological blocs, the document seems to be referring to attitudes that are *consciously* held and that structure concrete relationships of opposition, which the document calls sin only in an analogous sense.[15] There is a desire here to talk about contemporary situations of injustice and violence using the language of sin, and in *Sollicitudo rei socialis*, John Paul II states that the situation of the contemporary world cannot be properly analysed without reference to "structures of sin."[16] Yet despite his determination to employ the language of sin in order to bring such situations into the light of the gospel, the individual remains the basic unit of moral analysis: "It is a question," he says, "of *moral* evil, the fruit of *many sins* which lead to 'structures of sin.'"[17]

FALLING SHORT

It is here, I suggest, that we begin to see the effort involved in rearranging the conceptual planks and barrels of Catholic moral theology, and we also begin to see how those efforts fall short of their goal. The materials we have at hand simply cannot get us there. In traditional Catholic moral theology, the definition of formal sin resembles the following: a sin is an act offensive to or contrary to the laws of God, committed with knowledge that this is the case, and committed freely in that knowledge. Sin is always a particular some*thing* for which some*one* is responsible: it is always personal.

Significant difficulties arise when this understanding of sin is applied to social situations. If sin is always personal, it can pertain only to individuals and not to groups: groups, structures, social bodies, and systems simply cannot commit sins in the strict sense. Further, the more an act proceeds unconsciously from embedded social attitudes or systems, the less it is committed in full knowledge, and the more an act is compelled (or the more my options are constrained in choosing to undertake it), the less I can be said to do it freely.

Catholic moral theology develops the language of social sin in order to take account of how unjust social systems operate almost automatically or unconsciously, without the full awareness of those embedded in them. Yet, to the extent that a person's action is not free or conscious, that person is not culpable for it: the moral evil remains, but the essential elements of formal sin are attenuated. Conceptually speaking, social sin seems to cancel itself out. The more social the concept becomes—taking account of the automatic and unconscious ways in which systemic evil acts on moral agents—the less the activity of those moral agents appears as sin, traditionally understood. The more like sin it becomes—involving individually identifiable acts committed in freedom and knowledge—the less clearly its social and systemic dimensions appear. "Social" and "sin" appear to be two notions heading in opposite directions.

How does the Catholic social teaching square this circle? It keeps the individual as the basic unit of moral analysis and speaks of social sin or structures of sin in basically additive terms: structures of sin are the "fruit of many sins" or the result of the "accumulation and concentration of many personal sins," as we have seen. This has the advantage of safeguarding some principles profoundly important for Catholic social teaching—namely, the dignity and moral freedom of the human person. In situations of injustice and oppression, these are not principles we want to trade in for a stronger account of social sin's unconscious and systemic dimensions. But the difficulty here is that this move simply does not work: it does not provide us with an adequate understanding of what the social *is* or of the *relationship* between individuals and the social.

When John Paul II describes structures of sin as the "result" of the "accumulation and concentration of personal sins," two problems lurk in the background. The first is that the implied relationship between individuals and the social is one of part and whole, as though facts about the social could be explained by facts about the individuals comprising them. Second, the implied relationship between individuals and the social is one of cause and effect. In striving to avoid the view that the social straightforwardly produces individuals—a view that might lead to determinism and to people failing to take responsibility for sin by blaming it on "society"—Church teaching on social sin arguably leans too far the other way, toward the view that individuals straightforwardly produce the social. Sociologically or theologically, this simply does not work.

CRITICAL REALISM

It is here that Roy Bhaskar and critical realism can help us to describe social reality more accurately. In speaking about the social, as Bhaskar puts it, we are "not concerned, as such, with large-scale, mass or group behavior (conceived as the behavior of large numbers of individuals)" but rather "with the persistent *relations* between individuals (and groups) and with the relations between these relations and nature and the products of such relations."[18] Facts about social situations and social structures are not reducible to facts about individuals or about groups of individuals: social facts are facts about relationships. So, in the same way that it is not enough to explain social groups solely in terms of facts about the individuals comprising them, it is not enough to explain socially embedded situations of structural injustice and violence solely by means of the particular acts and attitudes of the individuals involved. Shortly before his death, Ignacio Martín-Baró, one of the Universidad Centroamericana Jesuits murdered by the Salvadoran security forces, wrote this about the violence engulfing the country:

Fundamentally, the problem is not one of isolated individuals whether few or many; it is a problem whose nature is strictly social. The damage that has been produced is not simply in the destruction of personal lives. Harm has been done to the social structures themselves—to the norms that order the common life, to the institutions that govern the life of citizens, to the values and principles by which people are educated and through which the repression has tried to justify itself.[19]

Accounting for social sin in terms of the "accumulation and concentration" of many personal sins does not do justice to its social dimensions, because the social itself cannot be exhaustively or straightforwardly accounted for by appeal to the accumulation and concentration of individuals comprising it.[20]

Bhaskar also helps us to locate the theological danger here. Social atomism—the idea that individuals straightforwardly produce the social—can lead us into a "voluntaristic idealism with respect to our understanding of social structure."[21] Although Bhaskar is addressing social scientists, this also applies to Catholic social teaching. If we describe social sin as the "accumulation and concentration" of personal sins, then the solution to it is simply personal conversion: we get rid of socially embedded injustice and violence by appealing to individuals. On one level this is right—the gospel *is* a call to radical personal conversion.[22] This is problematic when that call to conversion becomes a kind of social Pelagianism, as though the kingdom of God on earth were achievable if only individuals would act more virtuously. This kind of social Pelagianism can become a demand for an unrealistic kind of moral heroism, and, again, it risks misunderstanding the nature of social sin as it is concretely experienced. Writing about the embedded and enduring sectarian conflict in Northern Ireland, Joseph Liechty and Cecelia Clegg argue that

much thinking about sectarianism is faulty because we take a solely personal approach to a problem that is both personal and systemic. When thinking about sectarianism, we typically begin with personal attitudes and personal actions. Thus we absolve a person of responsibility, we think, when we say, "she doesn't have a sectarian bone in her body." In one sense, this concern with the personal is not only appropriate, we need more of it, not less. At the same time, however, too exclusively personal an approach fails to take seriously enough the systemic issues around sectarianism. To pose the problem another way: a sectarian system can be maintained by people who, individually, do not have a sectarian bone in their bodies.[23]

The problem is not one of wrong actions undertaken unconsciously or under compulsion—actions that, once the moral blindness involved in the situation is removed, can be recognized as wrong. The problem is that social relations in this context have become so persistently distorted that normal attitudes, innocent acts, and understandable choices—even *good* acts and attitudes—can maintain and perpetuate an unjust social fabric. It is thus, Liechty and Clegg suggest, that the sectarian system born from gross violence and what most people would now see as unapologetic injustice, can now maintain itself on a diet consisting largely of our rational responses, understandable comparisons, good intentions and positive actions.[24]

This systemic dimension is what the Church's teaching on social sin, as it stands, still struggles to address.

Catholic social teaching and moral theology have come a long way from the preconciliar manualist tradition, and the movement toward greater engagement with pressing social issues has been an important one. However, the rearrangement of the tradition's various planks and barrels that produces the understanding of social sin as an "accumulation and concentration of many personal sins" is not altogether successful. We need something in addition to the resources and key principles furnished by the theological tradition. I have suggested here that we might find that "something" in Roy Bhaskar and critical realism. The chapters that follow argue that borrowing critical realism can help us to bridge the gap, allowing Catholic social teaching and moral theology to reach a more satisfactory account of the way in which moral evil takes social shape.

NOTES

1. John O'Malley, *What Happened at Vatican II* (Cambridge, MA: Belknap Press, 2008), 53–92.
2. John A. Mahoney, *The Making of Moral Theology: A Study of the Roman Catholic Tradition* (Oxford: Clarendon Press, 1987), 31.
3. See James F. Keenan, *A History of Catholic Moral Theology in the Twentieth Century: From Confessing Sins to Liberating Consciences* (London: Continuum, 2010), 30.
4. Margaret R. Pfeil, "Doctrinal Implications of Magisterial Use of Language of Social Sin," *Louvain Studies* 27, no. 2 (2001), 132–52. The context was the attempt to retrieve the Lenten penitential practices of the early Church. See Vatican II, *Sacrosanctum concilium*, §109.
5. Vatican II, *Gaudium et spes*, §7, §25.
6. Vatican II, §25.
7. Consejo Episcopal Latinoamericano (CELAM), Medellín Conference Concluding Document (1968), §2–§5; and Puebla Conference Concluding Document (1979), §1032, §92, §281.
8. John Paul II, "The Value of This Collegial Body," in *Penance and Reconciliation in the Mission of the Church*, National Conference of Catholic Bishops (Washington, DC: USCCB, 1984).
9. John Paul II, *Reconciliatio et paenitentia* (1984), §16.
10. The document states in the previous paragraph, however, that "there is nothing so personal and untransferable in each individual as merit for virtue or responsibility for sin." John Paul II, *Reconciliatio et paenitentia*, §16.

11. In this vein, John Paul II refers to "social sins" including the drugs trade, corruption, and racism in the apostolic exhortation *Ecclesia in America*, §56.
12. John Paul II, *Reconciliatio et paenitentia*, §16. The 1979 US Bishops' 1979 pastoral letter, "Brothers and Sisters to Us," makes the same point concerning racism, but more boldly: "The structures of our society are subtly racist, for these structures reflect the values which society upholds. They are geared to the success of the majority and the failure of the minority; and members of both groups give unwitting approval by accepting things as they are. Perhaps no single individual is to blame. The sinfulness is often anonymous but nonetheless real. The sin is social in nature in that each of us, in varying degrees, is responsible. All of us in some measure are accomplices." Quoted in Mark O'Keefe, *What Are They Saying about Social Sin?* (Mahwah, NJ: Paulist Press, 1990), 66–67.
13. John Paul II, *Reconciliatio et paenitentia*, §16.
14. John Paul II, §16.
15. The CDF *Instruction on Christian Freedom and Liberation* talks in terms of a "secondary and derived sense" rather than an analogical sense. See CDF, *Instruction on Christian Freedom and Liberation* (Vatican City: Polyglott Press, 1986), §75.
16. John Paul II, *Sollicitudo rei socialis* (1987), §36.
17. John Paul II, §37. Emphasis in text.
18. Roy Bhaskar, *The Possibility of Naturalism: A Philosophical Critique of the Contemporary Human Sciences* (Brighton: Harvester Press, 1979), 35.
19. Ignacio Martín-Baró SJ, quoted in Margaret R. Pfeil, "Social Sin: Social Reconciliation?," in *Reconciliation, Churches and Nations in Latin America*, ed. Iain McLean, 171–89 (London: Ashgate, 2006), 184.
20. For more on this theme from a critical realist perspective, see Daniel Finn, "What Is a Sinful Social Structure?," *Theological Studies* 77, no. 1 (2016): 136–64.
21. Bhaskar, *Possibility of Naturalism*, 42.
22. Catholic social teaching on social sin clearly has the alternative possibility in view, for example, that imputing sin to impersonal societal structures or collectives allows individuals to deny responsibility. On this, see John Paul II, *Reconciliatio et paenitentia*, §16, and especially CDF, *Instruction on Christian Freedom and Liberation*, §74–§75.
23. Joseph Liechty and Cecelia Clegg, *Moving beyond Sectarianism: Religion, Conflict and Reconciliation in Northern Ireland* (Dublin: Columba Press, 2001), 9.
24. Liechty and Clegg, 14.

CHAPTER 3

What Is Critical Realism?

Daniel K. Finn

The primary contribution of critical realism to Christian ethics is an improved understanding of social structures and culture. In the next chapter, critical realist sociology explains how social structures alter our decisions and avoids both collectivism and individualism, respecting both human freedom and the powerful causal impact that structures have on the choices of persons acting within them. Chapter 5 does the same for culture.

However, these social scientific insights arise from and are warranted by more fundamental insights of critical realism in apprehending the natural world (i.e., concerning the natural sciences, the philosophy of science, and epistemology). Unlike scholars who insist that the social sciences are fundamentally different from natural science because they study human choice rather than atoms, molecules, or birds, critical realists make no special case for social science.[1] Yet, unlike empiricists, who limit our knowledge of the world to what our five senses can perceive, critical realists argue that even natural scientists aim to explain events by studying the often-invisible forces that cause them.

In the next chapter several of the conceptual tools employed in a critical realist understanding of natural science—emergence, the stratified character of reality, and the ontological reality of things that are not sense-perceptible—are available for use in social science.

EMERGENCE

The world is not flat but stratified. This is not a commentary on the shape of the Earth but on the character of both the natural and social worlds, and this insight predates critical realist philosophy.[2] Some parts of those worlds exist at a "higher" level than others, and emergence is the cause.

The simplest example of emergence is water, which exists at a "higher" level than do the oxygen and hydrogen atoms that combined to produce it. Water emerges from this combination of elements and is entirely dependent on them for its existence, yet it possesses characteristics that neither hydrogen nor oxygen does. Both of these will feed a fire, while water will extinguish it, a characteristic of water that is an "emergent property." The newly formed reality has characteristics that cannot be explained by the characteristics of those elements that combine to create it.

As Christian Smith explains, reality "exists and operates, in fact, on many levels, each of which is governed by structures, processes, and tendencies appropriate to its own level."[3] This is true from the smallest to the largest scale. Protons emerge from up quarks and down quarks under subatomic forces. Stars emit light because of the relation of various nuclear particles under extreme pressure and temperature in the star's core. As Michael Polanyi said half a century ago, "It is impossible to represent the organizing principles of a higher level by the laws governing its isolated particulars."[4] Roy Bhaskar, the British philosopher who founded critical realism, explained that "the operations of the higher level cannot be accounted for solely by the laws governing the lower-order level in which we might say the higher order level is 'rooted' and from which we can say it was 'emergent.'"[5]

The language of "higher" levels in natural and social reality does not, of course, refer to any spatial relationship or to any order of importance. It does, however, name widely recognized relationships among the "subatomic, atomic, molecular, chemical, biological, physiological, zoological, ecological, meteorological, mental, social, global, galactic, and cosmological."[6] The mechanisms and dynamics at one level are frequently different from those at other levels, and they often cause things to happen at that level which don't occur at either lower or higher levels.

For example, to understand even the simplest life-forms that first emerged from a slurry of inert chemicals on the Earth about 3.8 billion years ago, biologists have developed methods and paradigms quite different from those of chemists. And the emergence of human consciousness from the electrochemical processes of the brain has led psychologists to develop methods and paradigms different from those of biologists. Moreover, in some cases, the newly "emergent" entity has the capacity for "downward causation," in which it can have effects on elements at the lower level from which it emerged. Consciousness allows humans to have an effect on the brain, such as when a brain surgeon removes a cancerous tumor or a septuagenarian does the daily crossword puzzle to stay sharp.

Critical realist sociologists understand a social structure as emerging from the interaction of individual persons, but, having an ontological reality, it exercises a "downward" causal influence on those very individuals (see chapter 4). The phenomenon of emergence occurs in all areas of existence, and some emergents are sense-perceptible (e.g., water) and some are not (e.g., the human mind and social structures).

This view of emergence is not without controversy. Empiricist philosophers of science (and those practicing scientists who have adopted empiricist assumptions) are reductionist; they typically presume that any higher-level phenomenon can be explained by understanding the lower-level elements that combine to produce it. One classic statement of reductionism comes from Edward O. Wilson: "All tangible phenomena, from the birth of stars to the workings of social institutions, are based on material processes that are ultimately reducible, however long and tortuous the sequences, to the laws of physics."[7] Reductionism claims that "the causal power of the higher-level entity itself becomes redundant to the explanation."[8] Methodological individualists in the social sciences take a similar stand, seeing only persons and groups, not social structures, as the only causes in the social world.

This claim of reductionism—that all higher-level explanations can, in principle, be reduced to lower-level explanations—is often taken as a simple scientific fact. However, reductionism is a philosophical choice, not a scientific fact, and it is tied to the rise of empiricism in Western history.

PROBLEMS WITH EMPIRICISM

Empiricism is a theory asserting that, other than things that are true by definition, all knowledge arises from sense experience. This view has antecedents in the ancient world, but it came to full flowering in the work of John Locke and David Hume in the seventeenth and eighteenth centuries. That was an era when the Christian churches still understood biblical revelation as including scientific insight, and many intellectuals were keen to find a more reliable source of scientific knowledge than ancient religious understandings. The solution, developed most thoroughly at the time by Hume, was that science must be founded on the experiences of our five senses, with the help of definitional systems of thought like mathematics. For Hume, experience is "our only guide in reasoning concerning matters of fact."[9] Much that had historically been taken for real insight into the world had to be discarded. He dismissed religious thinking completely:

> If we take in our hand any Volume of Divinity or School Metaphysics, for Instance; let us ask, Does it contain any abstract Reasoning concerning Quantity or Number? No. Does it contain any experimental Reasoning concerning Matter of Fact and Existence? No. Commit it then to the Flames: For it can contain nothing but Sophistry and Illusion.[10]

Because of this epistemological limitation on what qualifies as knowledge, empiricism developed a conception of causality quite at odds with the everyday understanding of the average person. Limited to the sense-perceptible, empiricist causality could be nothing more than an invariable sequence of events. If event A always and unconditionally precedes event B, then A is the cause of B. John Stuart Mill helpfully described this empiricist limitation in his account of the views of Auguste Comte:

We have no knowledge of anything but phenomena. . . . We know not the essence, nor the real mode of production, of any fact, but only its relations to other facts in the way of succession or similitude. . . . Their essential nature, and their ultimate causes, either efficient or final, are unknown and inscrutable to us.[11]

A further implication is that scientific laws are then just statements about those invariable sequences of events. Sir Isaac Newton's inverse square law of gravity arises from the scientist's many experiments.

In the twentieth century, the dominant version of empiricism in the philosophy of science was provided by Carl Hempel's "covering law" model of scientific explanation.[12] An event can be explained if it can be logically deduced from a combination of (a) one or more scientific laws known to be true and (b) a set of circumstances that demonstrate that the law applies in this situation. The everyday result of all of this theoretical understanding of science and human knowledge is that, when I drop the book I am carrying, we say that it hits the floor because of the law of gravity.

THE CRITICAL REALIST ALTERNATIVE

Roy Bhaskar objected to the empiricist understanding of knowledge and science. He began with the claim that empiricism misconstrues what scientists do every day in the lab.

The exploratory power of a scientific experiment depends on the ability—often requiring great creativity—of scientists to eliminate from the "closed" situation of the scientific laboratory many of the influences that occur in the "open" situation of the world outside. To study gravity, for example, the physicist creates a vacuum in a long glass tube and then watches for any difference in the descent within the tube of a feather and of a pebble of equal weight. The empiricist explains that the invariability of the sequence of events substantiates the scientist's claims about gravity. But Bhaskar objects. On what grounds can the empiricist know that insights based on the invariable sequences discovered by the scientist in the closed situation of the lab will hold true in the open world outside the lab, where invariable sequences almost never occur?

The key here is that scientific experiments are not simple cases of a scientist "observing" invariable sequences. The scientist is "a causal agent of the sequence of events, but not of the causal laws which the sequence of events . . . enables us to identify."[13] What empiricism misses, Bhaskar argues, is that in science there are two types of knowledge based on the two objects of knowledge.

Two Types of Knowledge

Using a grammatical analogy, Bhaskar distinguishes between transitive and intransitive objects of knowledge. Transitive objects of knowledge are "the antecedently established facts and theories, paradigms and models, methods and techniques of inquiry available to a particular scientific school or worker."[14] Science is a human project, and Bhaskar explains that

> men in their social activity produce knowledge which is a social product much like any other, which is no more independent of its production and the men who produce it than motorcars, armchairs, or books, which has its own crafts-man, technicians, publicists, standards and skills and which is no less subject to change than any other commodity.[15]

Newton's inverse square law of gravity is a prime example of transitive knowledge: a human product, a scientist's attempt to name how things occur in the world.

Intransitive objects of knowledge are "the real things and structures, mechanisms and processes, events and possibilities of the world; and for the most part they are quite independent of us."[16] Newton's "law" of gravity is a human statement that points to real forces in the universe. For Bhaskar, it is *not* true that the book falls to the floor "because of the law of gravity." Rather, it is the relation between the book and the Earth that causes it to fall. Gravity is not a law but is instead a force. It is an emergent property of the relation between the book and the Earth.

The Reality of Transfactual Things

Empiricists deny our ability to know anything about the relation between the book and the Earth because that relation cannot be directly perceived by our five senses. Bhaskar argues that the scientist's experiments into the characteristics of gravity make sense only if they are exploring something that "really" happens in the world, exploring real relations that exist both inside and outside the lab. The relation between the book and the Earth is not sense-perceptible, but neither is a magnetic field. Scientists can indeed study and make observations and generalizations about these kinds of relations. Employing the empiricist's idea of a "fact" as something that is sense-perceptible, Bhaskar calls the relation between the book and the Earth "transfactual." Thus, contrary to empiricist doctrine, science itself makes little sense without admitting the ontological reality of things that are not sense-perceptible.

Although science thus attends to many things that are not observable, there is no mysticism involved. Like empiricists, critical realists understand the physicist to begin with the sense-perceptible, with carefully orchestrated observations in the laboratory. Moreover, they do not reject the statistical regressions of economists and political scientists.[17] However, they do aim for more than empiricist epistemological limitations would allow. As Christian Smith argues,

> Scientific inquiry as a project should be concerned more with the structured properties of causal relations and mechanisms than with the regularity of

observable sequences of events—theorizing unobserved causal dynamics is what the best of science actually does and is more important than measuring the strength of association between variables.[18]

Thus Bhaskar claims that empiricism is supported neither by the way science really works nor by the way working scientists understand what they are doing. Empiricists are guilty of "the epistemic fallacy." This is the error of reducing onto-logically real relations in the world to issues of human knowledge.[19] The ontologi-cally real relation between Earth and book is interpreted by empiricists as no more than a matter of our knowledge of its sense-perceptible consequences (that one event follows on another).

Three Domains of Reality

Finally, for our purposes in this brief introduction to critical realism, these insights into intransitive knowledge and the ontological reality of transfactual things lead Bhaskar to distinguish three "domains" of reality. The first is the "empirical," the sum total of all that is perceived. This includes not just the scientist's observa-tions in the lab but also your perception of the four chairs around your dining room table. The second is the "actual," which is the sum total of everything that occurs. This includes the empirical but also encompasses events that occur with-out anyone perceiving them, such as the fall of a rock down the side of one of the many unnamed mountains in Alaska. The third is the "real," all that exists. Reality includes the empirical and the actual, of course, but it also includes the causal forces—the powers or "mechanisms"—that bring about those events, including the relation between that Alaskan rock and the earth that causes the rock to descend the mountainside.

As Bhaskar summarizes scientific laws,

> Laws are then neither empirical statements (statements about experiences) nor statements about events. Instead, they are statements about the way of act-ing of independently existing and trans-factually active things.[20]

The law of gravity does not cause anything to happen. It is an (insightful) example of transitive knowledge that describes the force of attraction (which we call gravity) that emerges from the spatial relation of two physical bodies. As the next chapter explains, a similar insight is helpful in economics. Prices do not change "because of the law of supply and demand." Rather, what economists call the law of sup-ply and demand is but an insightful attempt to describe the dynamics that occur within the relation between social positions that constitute the market as a social structure when large numbers of people make choices to improve their economic well-being in the face of the constraints, opportunities, and incentives emergent in those markets. Scientific laws do not have causal force; they are human statements that point to causal forces in the world.

AN ASIDE CONCERNING CHRISTIAN FAITH

Like many other individuals of his era and since, David Hume made it clear that his rejection of Christian faith was closely tied to his epistemological convictions that we must not trust assertions about the world that cannot be tested by our five senses. As he cleverly put it,

> Upon the whole, we may conclude, that the Christian Religion not only was at first attended with miracles, but even at this day cannot be believed by any reasonable person without one.[21]

This conviction, rooted in empiricist philosophy of science, has become the predominant assumption about the relation of religion and science among intellectuals in the Western world over the last 250 years.

Still, there has been more criticism of empiricism in the last seventy years of the philosophy of science than there had been in the previous two centuries. If a critical realist perspective on science—with its affirmation of the ontological reality of unobservable things—were to prove persuasive to intellectuals more broadly, religious faith would attain an intellectual respectability, even among nonbelievers, that it has not enjoyed since Hume. As a result, critical realism has significant implications for Christian theology far beyond the borders of Christian ethics.[22]

CONCLUSION

This chapter provides a brief overview of critical realism as an account of scientific work, scientific knowledge, and the relation between our experience of natural events and the causes that bring them about.

Central here is the insight that the world, both natural and social, is stratified into different "levels." The cause of the stratification is the phenomenon of emergence, which occurs when two or more elements combine to produce something that has characteristics that cannot be adequately explained by the characteristics of the elements themselves.

Critical realism objects to the usual accounts of science provided by empiricism because those accounts describe neither what goes on in science nor what scientists understand themselves to be doing. Science generates transitive knowledge such as models and theories that are employed by scientists in their efforts to understand the world. The ultimate aim of science is to discover intransitive knowledge: understanding those forces and mechanisms—most frequently not sense-perceptible—that are the causes behind the events that scientists study.

This set of understandings entails a view of reality as made up of three domains: the empirical (everything that is perceived), the actual (everything that occurs, including but not limited to the empirical), and reality as a whole (including the empirical, the actual, and the transfactual forces that generate the events that occur).

This chapter's investigation into critical realist philosophy of science may seem at first to lie at a great distance from Christian ethics. However, these insights, when put to social scientific work in the next chapter, will generate a scientifically adequate understanding of the social world that will be of great benefit to ethical reflection on the difficulties of leading a responsible moral life within the many social structures where daily life occurs.

NOTES

1. Peter Winch, *The Idea of the Social Science and Its Relation to Philosophy* (London: Routledge, 1958); and Roy Bhaskar, *The Possibility of Naturalism: A Philosophical Critique of the Contemporary*, 4th ed. (London: Routledge, 2015).
2. Geoffrey M. Hodgson, "The Concept of Emergence in Social Science: Its History and Importance," *Emergence* 2, no. 4 (2000): 65–77.
3. Christian Smith, *What Is a Person? Rethinking Humanity, Social Life, and the Moral Good from the Person Up* (Chicago: University of Chicago Press, 2010), 34.
4. Michael Polanyi, *The Tacit Dimension* (New York: Doubleday, 1967), 36.
5. Roy Bhaskar, *A Realist Theory of Science* (Oxon: Routledge, 2008), 13.
6. Smith, *What Is a Person?*, 35.
7. Edward O. Wilson, *Sociobiology: The New Synthesis* (Cambridge, MA: Harvard University Press, 1975), 226.
8. Dave Elder-Vass, *The Causal Power of Social Structures: Emergence, Structure and Agency* (Cambridge: Cambridge University Press, 2010), 24.
9. David Hume, *An Enquiry concerning Human Understanding*, section 10: "Of Miracles, Part 1" (1748). First published as *Philosophical Essays concerning Human Understanding* in 1748, revised numerous times, and retitled in 1758, http://www.bartleby.com/37/3/15.html.
10. Hume, 256.
11. J. S. Mill, *Auguste Comte and Positivism*, 5th ed. (London: N. Trübner, 1907), 6.
12. For a description of "deductive-nomological" explanation, see Carl G. Hempel, *Aspects of Scientific Explanation: And Other Essays in the Philosophy of Science* (New York: Free Press, 1965), 335–76.
13. Bhaskar, *Realist Theory*, 33.
14. Bhaskar, 21.
15. Bhaskar.
16. Bhaskar, 22.

17. Douglas Porpora, "Do Realists Run Regressions?," in *After Postmodernism: An Introduction to Critical Realism*, ed. José López and Gary Potter (London: Athlone, 2001), 260–68.
18. Smith, *What Is a Person?*, 96.
19. Bhaskar, *Realist Theory*, 36–40.
20. Bhaskar, 52.
21. Hume, *Enquiry concerning Human Understanding*.
22. See, for example, Margaret Scotford Archer, Andrew Collier, and Douglas V. Porpora, *Transcendence: Critical Realism and God* (London: Routledge, 2004).

CHAPTER 4

Social Structures

Daniel K. Finn

Throughout its history, Christian ethics has recognized that the economic, political, and social situations in which Christians find themselves greatly complicate the challenge of living a responsible moral life. Theological assessments of these challenges varied widely in premodern Christian history. At a time of widespread cultural discouragement when eight centuries of continuous civil authority ended with the Visigoths' sack of Rome in 410, Augustine of Hippo outlined a pessimistic set of expectations for government and civic life in *The City of God*.[1] Eight centuries later, amid the greater hope of the High Middle Ages, Thomas Aquinas presented a more optimistic picture of what Christian faith might expect from both civil authority and secular knowledge.

Yet just as premodern biblical scholarship suffered from the lack of modern scientific insight into geology, biology, and astronomy, so too was premodern ethical reflection on social life limited by its ignorance of the insights into institutional life later provided by the development of the social sciences. In response to the modern awareness that economic, political, and social institutions can be subject to democratic reform, Christian theologians such as Walter Rauschenbusch, Abraham Kuyper, and Reinhold Niebuhr developed both critiques of social injustice and recommendations for reform. However, much has occurred in the social sciences since these great thinkers last put pen to paper.

Significant among such developments is critical realism, whose views on science, the philosophy of science, and epistemology are reviewed in chapter 3. This chapter summarizes the implications of critical realism for our understanding of social structures as developed by critical realist sociologists over the past forty years. Central here are treatments by Margaret Archer, Christian Smith, and Douglas Porpora of how social structures are ontologically real things that emerge from the actions of individuals, how they exist at a "higher" level than those individuals, and how the agency of persons interacts with the restrictions, opportunities, and incentives generated by structures. The chapter reviews the kind of power exercised by structures, why most persons within structures "go along" with restrictions and help to reproduce those structures, and how some persons, in an effort to transform structures, choose instead to ignore restrictions and "pay the price" those restrictions threaten.

Two final introductory observations are in order. First, although the focus in this chapter is on social structures, critical realist sociology also has much to say about culture and its relation to structure, as Matthew Shadle examines in chapter 5. Structure consists of objective relations among social positions, while culture consists of ideas, objects, and other things with meaningful content. Christian theology has long addressed culture but has mostly ignored social scientific analysis of structure.

Second, outsiders to science do indeed need to make choices among alternative perspectives presented by scientists. We noted in the last chapter how a reductionist view of human consciousness would leave us with the sense that human freedom is unreal and that the decisions of persons can be entirely explained, at least in principle, by the biology, chemistry, and ultimately the physics of the human brain. An analogous choice must be made among the alternative accounts of social life provided in sociology.

This primer is not the place for a full defense of the choice of critical realist sociology instead of the alternatives on offer in that discipline.[2] It is designed to introduce critical realism to those who have already decided to learn about it. Here we can simply note that some sociological perspectives are collectivistic (treating humans as little more than pawns pushed around on the chessboard of life by social forces), while others are individualistic (treating social life as nothing but the interactions of individual agents and groups). The first violates the Christian insight that persons are indeed free. The second amounts to "social Pelagianism," as Theodora Hawksley calls it in chapter 2. This second approach contradicts the long-standing awareness in the Christian tradition that economic, political, and social institutions are quite real (and sometimes understood as "organic") and can make leading a moral life far more difficult. Critical realism not only respects an appropriate tension between agency and structure but also articulates the tension in ways that are deeply helpful for Christian ethics in its effort to answer the challenge of living a responsible moral life within the structured world around us.

WHAT IS A SOCIAL STRUCTURE?

Douglas Porpora offers the basic definition of a social structure as "systems of human relations among social positions."[3] What, after all, are such social structures as a university or a parish or a city's traffic system or a convenience store or a chess club or a professional academic society? In each case, there needs to be particular material things, whether as complicated as a campus with buildings or as simple as three sets of chess pieces. Yet the core of a social structure is the system of relations among the various social positions that make it up.

In a university, the most fundamental relation is between the position of student and the position of professor in the classroom, but there are a host of other relations among social positions: student and fellow student, professor and department chair, assistant professor and the members of the committee on promotion and tenure, university president and employee, and so on. When we get on a city bus, we take on the position of rider in relation to the position of bus driver. And even so simple an institution as the chess club is constituted by the relation between member and member, member and president, and member and club secretary, who collects the dues.

HOW DO SOCIAL STRUCTURES OPERATE?

Two key insights follow. First, although the persons in these positions might have a *personal* relationship—I may ride the #13 bus to work every morning at the same time and greet Bill, the bus driver, when I enter and pay the fare—the key to understanding how the social structure of the transit system works is to realize that the social positions of rider and bus driver existed long before either Bill or I first entered into them. The same is true for people with doctoral degrees who enter into the position of college professor or others with high school diplomas who enter into the position of college students. The fundamentals of the relation (of bus rider and driver, of professor and students) are structural—that is, they are defined by the relation between preexisting social positions into which individual persons enter.

Second, like the invisible relation between the book and the Earth that generates the force we call gravity that causes the book to fall to the floor, the invisible relation between two social positions exerts causal impact on the persons who enter into them. In sociological terms, those relations between positions generate restrictions, "enablements" (i.e., opportunities), and incentives that shape the choices made by those who take on those positions.

When I take on the position of rider as I step onto the #13 bus, I face certain restrictions built into the relation between rider and driver: I should pay to enter the bus, I should not try to pay with French francs, I should not try to persuade the driver to alter the bus route, I should use earbuds instead of allowing my music to blare out to all, and so on. At the same time, as I take on the position of rider, I face certain opportunities: I get to be transported to my workplace, I have the option of exiting early or staying on the bus to the end of the route, I get to read and avoid the hassles of driving in rush hour, and so on. These objective restrictions and opportunities are perceived by me psychologically as incentives (or disincentives).

Critical realists go on to explain the relation between agency and structure. Only persons have agency, even though structures have powerful causal impact. Persons continue to have freedom, continue to make choices within structures to accomplish whatever goals they may have. Yet because the social structure generates restrictions, opportunities, and incentives, those decisions are often different from what they would otherwise have been.

As a bus rider, I might prefer not to use earbuds when listening to music, but the restriction against this on the bus leads most riders to listen quietly. There is no determinism here. If I wished, I could listen without the earbuds, but the existence of the restriction entails the fact that I would pay a price. The bus driver might intervene (perhaps even insisting that I leave the bus if I persist), although before that the relation between rider and rider would likely come into play, with my fellow riders giving me dirty looks or speaking up to object. Similarly, in the relation between the position of student and the position of professor in the classroom, students remain free not to complete assignments or to skip exams, but they will pay a price (a lower grade or even failing the course) if they make such choices. Professors do not *have* to strive to make their classes interesting, but they will pay a price if they don't (student disapproval or perhaps a negative pre-tenure review). Most of us, most of the time, "go along" with the restrictions we face within social structures. Thus, for example, one of the signs of a good job is that the person who holds the position is not bothered by the restrictions it entails. Additional examples of how structures influence our choices are provided in David Cloutier's chapter 6 (on the environment) and Matthew Shadle's chapter 7 (on the economy).

WHAT IS THE ADVANTAGE FOR CHRISTIAN ETHICS?

The insight provided here by critical realist sociologists that is most helpful to Christian ethics is the awareness that social structures affect moral agency. Our day is filled with restrictions, opportunities, and incentives generated within social structures that do indeed shape our choices. Whether buying a tank of gas, watching a child's soccer game, listening to a pastor's sermon, deciding whether to rob a bank, paying for lunch at a restaurant, attending a meeting, or driving no more than five miles per hour over the speed limit, our decisions to do this or not do that are profoundly influenced by the objective restrictions and opportunities we face. These do not violate our freedom since there is no determinism entailed here. Yet the analysis does name more precisely and more realistically the context of our freedom, the constraints in our freedom, identifying the causal impacts that social structures do indeed have on our choices. Whether the impact of particular social structures is morally beneficial or destructive is central to Christian ethics and fundamental for the moral life of individual persons.

In an ideal world, all of the restrictions we face throughout the day would make it more difficult for us to act in sinful ways, and all the opportunities presented to us would lead us to choose what is morally good. However, since both we and the world around us are subject to sin, finitude, and ignorance, the structures within which we live all too frequently threaten personal morality and the common good by placing restrictions on (thus penalizing) virtuous behavior and presenting opportunities for (thus promoting) vice. Changing such structures will be less challenging if we understand how they work.

EMERGENCE, REPRODUCTION, AND
TRANSFORMATION OF SOCIAL STRUCTURES

Social structures emerge from the actions of individual persons. In general, there is no identifiable original decision to create a social structure, as is obvious with the government of the United Kingdom, the traffic system of Paris, the market for flowers in the Netherlands, the system of peer review within the natural sciences, or a college to educate young adults. Sometimes a conscious decision creates an organization, as when the Board of the Massachusetts Bay Colony voted in 1636 to create a "New College" in Cambridge. Yet even this new organization was to include the relations among social positions that had existed in colleges back in England. The social structure called "a college" had long been in existence. No one starts a new organization without facing restrictions and opportunities within social structures already in existence. As Margaret Archer has argued, "people . . . either reproduce or transform structure, rather than creating it."[4] "This is the human condition, to be born into a social context (of language, beliefs and organization) which was not of our making: agential power is always restricted to re-making whether this be reproducing or transforming our social inheritance."[5] In Bhaskar's words, "Society stands to individuals then as something that they never make, but that exists only in virtue of their activity."[6]

Just as water cannot exist without the hydrogen and oxygen that combine to form it, so social structures cannot exist without the ongoing participation of persons within them. Typically, those persons "go along" without much of a fuss, living within the restrictions and taking advantage of the opportunities they face.

Still, unpredictability is always present. Even if there is an identifiable originating decision for an organization, things rarely turn out as their founders intended. Structures emerge from the interactions of persons with varying goals, and the actions of those persons are influenced in turn by the structures themselves. That new college in Massachusetts was named Harvard three years after its founding due to a £780 bequest a year earlier arising from the death of thirty-year-old John Harvard. And neither the members of the Colony Board nor Mr. Harvard, devout Christians as they all were, could have imagined the secular institution that is Harvard University today.

Of course, not everyone will "go along." Different groups within a social structure face different sets of restrictions and opportunities. Anyone in a social structure can undertake its transformation, but it is rare that those who are privileged (who have the fewest restrictions and the most opportunities) begin this process. Most often, it is persons facing significant restrictions who press for change. Violating restrictions means those persons will pay a price, and it is most often only those with least to lose who take the risk. Although it is exceedingly difficult to change social structures, examples of successful efforts are many. On a large scale, these include the labor movements of the first half of the twentieth century, the civil rights movements of the second half, and, still unfolding, the campaign to unionize contingent university faculty at the beginning of the twenty-first century. On a smaller scale, there are the efforts of parishioners to alter the budget priorities of their congregation, and of a member of the bowling league to adjust the Tuesday evening start time by thirty minutes.

CONSTRICTIVE AND ENTICIVE POWER

Out of a concern for the abuses committed by powerful persons and institutions in the lives of so many people around the world, some Christian ethicists talk as if power is evil and say they want to reduce the influence of power in life. However, as philosopher Thomas Wartenberg has persuasively argued, power is just as frequently a positive force.[7] Parents exercise power over their toddlers, police officers keep citizens behind the yellow tape at a murder scene, courts issue subpoenas to drug lords, store managers fire employees who do not show up for work, and many a playground monitor has prevented that big kid from bullying little Billy.

More to the point, the restrictions and opportunities that are generated by the relation between social positions in any social structure are examples of power. In no situation is power the only reality at work. In well-functioning families, workplaces, cities, and clubs, power is in the background, not frequently divisive, and often not part of daily consciousness.

Restrictions and Constrictive Power

Think of the structurally generated restrictions that forbid students from cheating on an exam, cashiers from pilfering money from the cash drawer, bus riders from letting their music blare out for all to hear, drivers from speeding, or library patrons from speaking in a loud voice. In each case, the restriction is a threat, a conditional penalty: if you do X, you will pay price Y. Five things are critical to notice in each of these cases.

First, the restriction arose for any particular person because they entered into a preexisting social position that was already in relation to other social positions, and the restrictions were generated by the relation. Second, these restrictions constrain but do not cancel the freedom of the persons involved. The driver is free to speed, and the bus rider can choose to let the music blare. Third, the severity of the penalty—how serious Y is—varies greatly. A dishonest cashier could end up in jail; the loud library patron might get no more than a disapproving look from others nearby. Fourth, the power involved here is not just a person-to-person phenomenon. The person who presents the threat is typically not the principal enforcer of the penalty. The college professor, the convenience store manager, the bus driver, the state patrol officer, and the librarian exercise power because of the positions they occupy. Yet that power, as Wartenberg argues, is dependent upon "aligned social agents," other persons in other social positions who will implement the penalty Y.[8] Fifth, unlike the examples so far, restrictions can be destructive, morally or in other ways. College professors can penalize students whose political views differ from their own, managers can penalize subordinates who complain about inefficient departmental procedures, and dictators can forbid citizens from forming political parties. Power can be morally positive or negative.

The point here is that the "logic" of power in differing structural restrictions — what we might call "constrictive power" — is the same: a conditional penalty. If you do X, you will pay price Y.

Opportunities and Enticive Power

Social structures exert power in the imposition of restrictions but also in the provision of opportunities. Parallel to restrictions as conditional penalties, opportunities are conditional rewards. If you do X, you will have reward Y. This is the power of enticement.

Consider the opportunities that structures can provide. The salesman can earn a bonus if he exceeds his sales goals for the year, the army private can be promoted to corporal if she excels at her duties, the assistant professor can get university funding to attend a conference if she presents a paper there, and a Boy Scout earns a merit badge if he demonstrates the appropriate knowledge and skill. People in powerful positions are often perceived as the source of such power, and they do have a degree of discretion, but the power of the powerful almost always arises from the social positions they hold in a social structure, and it is the relations between social positions that both constitute the structure and generate the power. As with restrictive power, there are five things to note here.

First, the opportunity arose for any particular person because they entered into a preexisting social position that was already in relation to other social positions, and the opportunity was generated by the relation. Second, the social structures that generate these opportunities entice action but do not force it; they do not cancel the freedom of the persons involved. The salesman is free to ignore the bonus offered and the assistant professor can ignore the funding available. Third, the importance of the reward — how significant Y is — varies greatly. An additional merit badge earned by an Eagle Scout may not mean much, but the salesman's year-end bonus may be the way he and his wife can afford their daughter's college tuition. Fourth, the power involved in opportunities is not just a person-to-person phenomenon. The person who presents the conditional reward typically does not provide it. The sales team manager, the army captain, the department chair, and the Boy Scout leader exercise power because of the positions they occupy, but that power, here too, is dependent upon aligned social agents, other persons in other social positions who will participate in the provision of the reward Y. Fifth, unlike the examples so far, opportunities can be destructive, morally or in other ways. Casinos can encourage addiction by offering special deals to gamblers who visit frequently; donors can subvert the character of a university by offering multimillion-dollar gifts to establish programs with ideological constraints;

and businesses can undermine public trust by offering bribes to government purchasing officers. The power of opportunities can be morally positive or negative.

As with restrictions, the "logic" of power in structural opportunities—what we might call "enticive power"—is the same: a conditional reward. If you do X, you will receive reward Y. Enticive power is less objectionable to those subject to it than is constrictive power because it can be ignored—simply by forgoing the opportunity offered. Opportunities are optional. Yet like constrictive power, it is a causally influential feature of daily life within social structures. We all have had the experience of buying something "because" it was on sale. The opportunity is not the only cause, but it certainly has causal impact.

These insights are helpful in a wide variety of issues in Christian ethics. Consider the example of economic markets, explored by Matthew Shadle in chapter 7. We can now understand markets as social structures—systems of relations among social positions—that influence the choices of both consumers and producers by means of restrictions and opportunities presented by prices, legal and cultural rules for markets, and other characteristics of economic relations. The "law" of supply and demand does not cause prices to change any more than the "law" of gravity causes the book to fall to the floor. Rather, the "law" points to the real economic forces at work—the power of (changing) threats and enticements that market relations generate.

In sum, there are two kinds of power operative in social structures: constrictive and enticive. Constrictive power operates by a threat, a conditional penalty; enticive power operates by an opportunity, a conditional reward. Only persons are conscious agents, but social structures have their influence on the choices those agents make through the constrictive power of restrictions and the enticive power of opportunities that those structures generate. From kindergarten teacher to the world's greatest tyrant, power over others is both constrictive and enticive. And in both forms it can be exercised for good or ill.

POWERFUL PERSONS

There is a widespread but mistaken tendency to think that power is just a possession of powerful persons. Almost always, however, powerful persons exercise power because of the social position they have taken on in some social structure. The insights of critical realism into structure and of Thomas Wartenberg into the exercise of power are helpful in sorting out the issues.

Consider the chief executive (CEO) of a multinational firm, or the mayor of a large city, or the president of a university. On the one hand, these influential people get to make important decisions that offer opportunities or present restrictions to others. The fact that they have considerable discretion in making those decisions leads us to prefer some candidates for those positions over others. The competence, values, temperament, and "philosophy" of the various candidates for such offices make a significant difference.

On the other hand, the power that these people exercise is not just theirs. First, as we have seen, those who, we say, "have power" depend on others to enforce the restrictions or implement the opportunities that power entails. Second, such power arises from the relations of the preexisting positions (of CEO, mayor, or president) to other social positions within and even outside the organizations they lead. For example, the enticive power to locate a new factory at any of three competing sites exists because the firm's board of directors has invested the position of CEO with this authority.

Third, even powerful people make their decisions in the light of restrictions, opportunities, and incentives that they face, which would be faced by anyone in their position. Some of those restrictions, for example, are enforceable by law and the courts. Others have less severe but still significant enforcement mechanisms. Like anyone else in an organization, if they choose to violate a restriction, they will pay a price—ranging from loss of support (e.g., if the student body protests an unfavorable presidential decision) to loss of a job (e.g., if the board of directors judges the CEO to have failed).

Influential people are free, of course, to ignore the restrictions and opportunities they face, just like everyone else in the social structure. But those responsible for appointing people to important positions typically research the background of all candidates carefully and appoint only those inclined to sustain rather than challenge the organization they are called upon to lead.

In sum, there are indeed powerful people in the world, but that power almost always arises not from their personal attributes but from the fact that they have taken on a powerful position within a social structure. The more precise account of the operation of social structures provided by Wartenberg and critical realist sociology provides Christian ethics with a structural understanding of power, thereby avoiding individualistic misunderstandings.[9]

VIRTUE IN PERSONS AND SOCIAL STRUCTURES

This discussion of restrictions, opportunities, incentives, and power has thus far ignored the question of the virtue of the persons facing them. Chapter 8, by Daniel Daly, addresses this issue in more detail, but for now we can observe that virtue makes a big difference (as does vice, of course).

Relating Structure and Morality

Restrictions and opportunities shape human choice, but they do not determine it. At their best, they make virtuous action more likely; at their worst, they make it less so. Even when restrictions penalize bad choices and opportunities reward good ones, we hope that people choose the moral course of action out of principle, not only because of the structure's effect. And when structures penalize good choices and opportunities reward bad ones, we hope that virtuous persons acting within those structures will resist the restrictions and forgo the opportunities. These insights into structures and morality were foreshadowed by the premodern moral assessment of law. Although they differ among themselves, Aristotle, Augustine, Aquinas, Martin Luther, and many others gave credit to "law" in its power to restrain vice.

When structures penalize moral actions, of course, virtuous agents will pay a price for their courage. Sometimes the price is high. The Czech writer and philosopher Václav Havel was imprisoned for years for opposing the Communist government before its fall in 1989 and his election as president of his nation. However, a price may be paid, though a much smaller one, even by the secretary who points out the inefficiency of the boss's latest office policy concerning the departmental photocopier.

Thinking only of the efficiency of an organization, the ideal situation is where restrictions penalize actions that run counter to the organization's goals and where opportunities elicit actions that contribute to those goals. Thinking morally, in well-structured organizations, restrictions penalize vice whereas opportunities encourage virtue. Efficiency and morality need not coincide. The Mafia may be both efficient and immoral. The local food pantry for the poor may be moral but inefficient.

Improving Social Structures

An advantage that the critical realist understanding of social structures brings to Christian ethics is not only a sharper identification of how structures have their impact. Once we recognize that it is through restrictions and opportunities (perceived as incentives) that structures have their impact for good or ill, procedures for improving the justice of structures come into view.

The starting point is to identify what *are* the operative restrictions and opportunities facing different groups in any particular social structure. And the best way to find that out is to ask the people involved. Thus, for example, the faculty members of the department of theology should meet to first identify—and then discuss the warrants for—the differing restrictions and opportunities facing different groups within the department. Junior and senior faculty, contingent and tenured/tenure-track faculty, men and women, and different racial and ethnic groups may point to the most pressing lines of division, but other ways of defining groups may identify morally relevant differences as well. The different restrictions and opportunities facing different subgroups may be morally and organizationally appropriate—or not. This process does not provide the moral answers (critical realism does not substitute for moral analysis) but it does raise the questions—questions usually avoided by those facing the fewest restrictions and most opportunities (another way of saying "the privileged"), who typically control the agenda.

Of course, the next conversation ought not to be limited to the faculty. A discussion of differences faced by office staff and faculty may be revealing. Similarly, everyone who works in or for the department would be significant candidates for inclusion in a similar conversation: the men and women who empty the waste-baskets, vacuum the carpets, and clean the toilets.

Such a conversation can take place not just at our place of work but at the committee we serve on in our congregation and at the United Way board where we serve as a member. Moreover, if this insight into the working of structures gains prominence, we can insist upon such conversations as a standard of elementary justice within organizations of all types. In large organizations, these will be conversations among representatives of different groups. Of course, the privileged may refuse to participate.

The final step—changing the restrictions and opportunities—is never simple, but this conversation process requires the privileged to give reasons for their advantage. If they agree that certain restrictions or opportunities should be changed, the larger group can decide on ways to accomplish the transformation. If they insist on retaining their advantages, often with the argument that they themselves are subject to restrictions and thus cannot change "the system," the process will at least have clarified the issues and allowed a challenge to the rationale they provide. As always, morally significant change may require the violation of restrictions to bring about transformation resisted by the privileged.

AN ASIDE ON COLLECTIVE AGENCY

We have stressed throughout this chapter that only persons are agents but that social structures exercise powerful influence on those agents through the restrictions, opportunities, and incentives that they generate. Still, it is evident in our globalized world that some of the most influential actors are large national or multinational organizations. Should we ascribe some form of agency to a business corporation or a national government or other large organization? Given the scope of this primer, we cannot resolve the question. Yet two observations are in order.

The first is that this is an issue under debate among critical realist sociologists. Part of the problem, of course, is the English word "agent." Sociologists typically use the word "agent" as a rough synonym for a person capable of making choices. But chemists also talk about some chemicals as agents, employing the word to refer to anything which is a cause, anything that produces an effect. Employing the understanding of agency as entailing the capacity to make choices, there are still competing alternatives available. The first and apparently dominant view among critical realist sociologists is that while we can speak of Exxon or Facebook as corporations "doing" things, all their decisions are made and announced by persons, typically corporate officers, who have taken on positions of authority within them. The other view is that some sort of collective agency emerges from the interaction of such persons in authority.

The second observation, however, puts this question of collective agency into perspective: it is a minor issue amid the major contribution that the critical realist view of structure has to contribute to Christian ethics. The summary statement that only persons are agents well describes 99.99 percent of the effects that structures have in our lives. Whether you are working at Exxon, updating your Facebook page, buying a loaf of bread, listening to an evening lecture, deciding whether to cheat a customer, coaching your daughter's basketball team, serving a meal to the homeless, choosing a cruising speed on the interstate, or backpacking in Yosemite National Park, the restrictions, opportunities, and incentives by which social structures influence your choices are not themselves agents. And the primary contribution that critical realist sociology can make to Christian ethics is an understanding of how our daily choices, made in freedom, are nonetheless profoundly shaped—for good or ill—by the social structures within which we live.

CONCLUSION

Critical realist sociology provides to Christian theology an insightfully precise way to understand how it is that social structures have causal impact on the decisions of individuals within them without canceling individual freedom. A social structure emerges from the interactions of persons and has an ontological reality at a "higher" level than those persons, influencing their choices by means of the restrictions, opportunities, and incentives it generates. Restrictions are a form of constrictive power and opportunities a form of enticive power. Both forms of power have causal impact in the lives of persons within social structures.

Most frequently, persons "go along" with the restrictions and opportunities they face, thus contributing to the reproduction of the social structure. Nonetheless, some persons—typically those with fewer opportunities and more restrictions—pay the price of violating restrictions in an effort to transform the social structure.

A better understanding of how structures shape human choice opens the possibility for a more transparent recognition of whether the restrictions, opportunities, and incentives in a particular structure serve the goals we hold. Those goals might be completely functional. Do the complications of reporting a problem with the company's website discourage employees from making the effort? More importantly for Christian ethics, those goals might entail personal morality. Does the opportunity to defraud the company without detection entice an account manager to embezzlement? Or the goals might concern global environmental responsibility. Do the restrictions of the oil company's chief executive against reporting quarterly losses lead the vice president in charge of drilling to forgo maintenance needed to avoid a catastrophic oil spill? Alternatively, the goals might focus on the quality of human relations. Does the hiring of three assistant professors for only two eventual tenured positions tempt the three to destructive forms of competition?

These insights into how social structures influence human choice will not resolve most of the enduring debates within Christian ethics. For example, we need an assessment of the moral responsibility for decisions made by persons facing constrictive power. Wartenberg judges that an agent subject to socially situated power is not fully responsible for what she does since she wanted to do something else.[10] To what *extent* is she responsible? Much work in ethics remains to be done, but by avoiding the errors of collectivism on the left and individualism on the right, these insights into structure will lead to more transparent conversations about the proper moral warrants for structural advantage and to more effective efforts to transform destructive social structures.

Still, as we noted earlier, social structures make up only half the social world. Culture is equally important, and the critical realist understanding of culture has much to contribute to Christian moral deliberation, as the next chapter explains.

NOTES

1. Augustine of Hippo, *City of God* (New York: Modern Library, 1950).
2. For a brief outline of the alternatives in sociology and their problems from the perspective of Christian theology, see Daniel K. Finn, "What Is a Sinful Social Structure?," *Theological Studies* 77, no. 1 (March 2016): 136–64.
3. Douglas V. Porpora, "Four Concepts of Social Structure," *Journal for the Theory of Social Behavior* 19, no. 2 (1989): 195.
4. Margaret Archer, *Realist Social Theory: The Morphogenetic Approach* (Cambridge: Cambridge University Press, 1995), 71.
5. Archer, 72.
6. Roy Bhaskar, *The Possibility of Naturalism: A Philosophical Critique of the Contemporary*, 4th ed. (London: Routledge, Taylor and Francis Group, 2015), 34.
7. Thomas E. Wartenberg, *The Forms of Power: From Domination to Transformation* (Philadelphia: Temple University Press, 1990), 11–12.
8. Wartenberg, 169.
9. For a more detailed discussion of the relation of roles and the particular persons inhabiting them, see Margaret Archer, *Realist Social Theory*, 186–88.
10. Wartenberg, *Forms of Power*, 86.

CHAPTER 5

Culture

Matthew A. Shadle

Nearly all the leading Catholic theologians of the past century spoke of the importance of culture for living out Christian faith and for understanding it theologically. Hans Urs von Balthasar spent his life, many say, working to unite faith and culture.[1] Bernard Lonergan defined Christian theology as the mediation between Christian faith and culture—that is, working out what faith means in the context of the culture of a particular time and place.[2] If the task of theology requires engagement with culture, then it is incumbent on theologians to understand culture well. This is particularly true for moral theology, where an appreciation for the influence of culture on moral agency is central.

This chapter introduces critical realism's understanding of culture, focusing in particular on the work of British sociologist Margaret S. Archer. It also provides an overview of some of the areas of theology where the notion of culture plays a key role and then examines how critical realism can help theologians working in these areas.

THEOLOGY AND CULTURE

The Second Vatican Council represents a pivotal moment in Christian theological engagement with culture. The Council's "Pastoral Constitution on the Church in the Modern World," *Gaudium et spes*, devotes an entire chapter to culture. It seriously engages with the notion of culture that had been developed by anthropologists earlier in the century: a system of beliefs, values, and customs shared by a distinct group of people. This understanding of culture differed from the earlier notion of "high culture" that distinguished the "cultured" or "civilized" person or society from the "uncivilized" or "barbaric."[3] *Gaudium et spes* defines culture as the "different styles of life and multiple scales of values [that] arise from the diverse manner of using things, of laboring, of expressing oneself, of practicing religion, of forming customs, of establishing laws and juridic institutions, of cultivating the sciences, the arts, and beauty."[4] And, as Robert Tucci notes, the document recognizes the diversity of cultures that have "different features and forms" and rejects a more hierarchical "aristocratic conception of culture."[5]

The Council's purpose in addressing the issue of culture is to better understand the relationship between the Gospel and the diverse cultures of the world. On the one hand, *Gaudium et spes* teaches that the Gospel has a purifying role in relation to culture.

> The Gospel of Christ constantly renews the life and culture of fallen man, it combats and removes the errors and evils resulting from the permanent allurement of sin. It never ceases to purify and elevate the morality of peoples. By riches coming from above, it makes fruitful, as it were from within, the spiritual qualities and traditions of every people of every age. It strengthens, perfects and restores them in Christ.[6]

On the other hand, the document also claims that people encounter the Gospel in and through their particular culture: "God, revealing Himself to His people to the extent of a full manifestation of Himself in His Incarnate Son, has spoken according to the culture proper to each epoch."[7] The church, "living in various circumstances in the course of time, has used the discoveries of different cultures" in its preaching and liturgical worship, and, significantly, the Council asserts that the church draws on culture to "more deeply understand" and "give . . . better expression" to the message of Christ with which it has been entrusted.[8]

Christian theology engages with the notion of culture in a number of ways suggested by *Gaudium et spes*. For example, the church's evolving response to secularization and pluralism raises important questions about the church's relationship to culture. Although these phenomena have raised important *political* questions for Christians over the decades—most importantly the issues of religious liberty and democratic participation—they also provoke important cultural questions. The process of secularization has involved the transformation of society from a Christian culture in which a sense of the sacred pervaded all of life to one in which religion has become a distinct social sphere differentiated from other spheres of life.[9] Likewise, the pluralization of society—the diversification of religious beliefs, worldviews, and lifestyles—has accelerated in recent decades as a result not only of secularization but also the flow of people and information resulting from globalization. The church faces serious questions about how to understand the relationship between Christian faith and the increasingly pluralistic cultures in which it finds itself.

A second important way in which Christian theology engages with culture is through inculturation or contextualization.[10] This process entails the adaptation of the church's teaching, worship, and social practice to local cultures as well as the methodological process of using local cultures as both objects of reflection and source materials for theology. The adaptation of the Gospel to local cultures has a long tradition (illustrated, for example, in the work of the Jesuits Matteo Ricci in China and Roberto Nobili in India in the sixteenth and seventeenth centuries), and more systematic reflection on the process of inculturation began in the field of missiology in the twentieth century. By the later decades of that century, however, the sense emerged that inculturation is not just a tool for communicating the Gospel to those who have not heard it but indeed a necessary embodiment of the church as a communion reflecting diversity in unity. As the Hong Kong theologian Mary Mee-Yin Yuen notes, "The one and universal Church is realized in and through the variety of local churches," each of which is called to a process of dialogue with the particular culture of its people.[11] The contributions of these local cultures enrich the universal church and its understanding of the faith.

A third area in which theology engages with culture is through the critique of unjust cultural systems and practices, exemplified in the diverse forms of liberation theology. The Latin American liberation theology that emerged in the late 1960s and early 1970s primarily offered a theological critique of the political and economic systems at the national and global levels that oppressed the poor. Other forms of liberation theology, however, have focused more on culture. For example, black liberation theology in the United States, also beginning in the late 1960s, has focused not only on the political and economic oppression of African Americans but also on the cultural construction of race. Feminist theology examines the cultural construction and reproduction of gender roles, critiquing Christianity's part in supporting restrictive roles while also offering a theological vision of women's flourishing.

All three of these forms of engagement between theology and culture—responding to secularization and pluralism, adapting the Gospel through inculturation, and critiquing unjust cultural systems and practices—require theologians to have an adequate understanding of culture. Critical realism offers a set of tools to help theologians better understand the nature of culture, how it shapes us and our actions, and how it can be transformed. It therefore can serve as a useful ally for theologians engaged in any of the tasks outlined above.

PROBLEMS WITH THE PREVALENT
VIEW OF CULTURE

In one of the best treatments of the relationship of theology and culture, Episcopalian theologian Kathryn Tanner outlines the main elements of what she calls the "modern meaning of culture" developed by early twentieth-century anthropologists like Franz Boas, Ruth Benedict, and Claude Lévi-Strauss. She argues that many elements of the modern meaning of culture are positive and insightful. First of all, in this view, culture is a universal characteristic of humankind; that is, all people share in one culture or another. In addition, different people participate in different cultures, and the diversity of cultures divides people into distinct social groups. According to the modern meaning of culture, culture encompasses a social group's entire way of life and is shared by all members of that social group, establishing a form of social consensus. Culture gives form to the relatively plastic biological instincts and capacities of human nature. Cultures are human constructions, and therefore they are contingent. Finally, although cultures are contingent, participants in a culture are unavoidably shaped by that culture.[12]

This modern understanding of culture represents a significant advance in our anthropological understanding of human cultures and has been of great use to theologians seeking to trace the relationship between faith and culture. Nonetheless, Tanner helpfully identifies several ways in which it distorts our understanding of culture. First, it downplays the contradictions, disagreements, and diversity within a single culture. Advocates of the modern view see cultures as coherent systems of meaning, but Tanner, drawing on the work of contemporary anthropologists, insists that cultures often exhibit internally contradictory values and beliefs. Likewise, the modern understanding of culture proposes that cultures are a source of social cohesion and consensus, but Tanner points out that within a particular social group, there is often contention and disagreement over the group's identity, norms, and values. Similarly, she explains that these disagreements often lead to social conflict and changes in a given culture, whereas the modern view of culture tends to downplay conflict and change over time. Finally, she proposes that, although cultures do distinguish one social group from another, the boundaries between them should not be seen as impermeable; rather, there is a constant process of interchange between distinct cultures.[13] Tanner's criticisms of prevalent understandings of culture are well taken, but her critique would be greatly strengthened if she had access to a more adequate understanding of culture, as would other theologians who share her concerns. It is the thesis of this volume that Christian ethicists and Christian theologians of all kinds can gain precision in addressing such issues by employing a more adequate sociological approach.

Margaret S. Archer, one of the leading proponents of critical realist sociology, has critiqued what she calls "the myth of cultural integration" that is characteristic of much of modern anthropological and sociological thinking about culture. Like Tanner, Archer criticizes the notion that cultures necessarily provide their participants a coherent pattern of thinking, with no internal contradictions. Similarly, she disputes the notion that cultures by definition imply a type of social consensus or cohesion.[14] This chapter proposes that critical realism can provide a more adequate way of thinking about culture, one that accounts for conflict within cultures as well as the changes cultures experience over time. The rest of this chapter explores the critical realist perspective on culture and why it would be valuable to theologians who address questions related to culture in their work.

CRITICAL REALISM AND CULTURE

Archer notes that the notion of culture has remained underdeveloped in the field of sociology. Although sociologists have given a great deal of attention to structure, their understanding of culture remains "inordinately vague" and their elaboration of how culture functions suffers from a "poverty of conceptualization."[15]

The more satisfactory view of culture she proposes arises out of the critical realist framework addressed in chapters 3 and 4. She proposes that, although culture and structure need to be carefully distinguished, the conceptual framework critical realists have developed to understand how social structures affect human agency can be adapted to gain insight into how culture functions as well. Structures are those features of social life that condition and constrain human behavior that are characterized by "primary dependence upon material resources, both physical and human."[16] Structures therefore would include things like the distribution of material resources, the power people are subject to in organizations, the balance between different sectors of the economy (e.g., agriculture, industry, service), and the demographic makeup of a population. Culture, on the other hand, refers to the entire "world of ideas" available to a social group at a given time.[17] The elements of culture are "intelligibilia," meaningful things, including ideas, beliefs, symbols, games, and even many objects, including statues or stop signs.[18]

As with structures, "cultural factors ultimately emerge from people and are efficacious only through people."[19] And having emerged, culture, like social structures, exists at a "higher level" than those people and has "temporal priority, relative autonomy and causal efficacy *vis-à-vis* members of society."[20] Like structures, culture has its causal impact in a nondeterministic way; persons are free to reject this or that part of culture, although in most cases one's culture is accepted simply as a part of "the way things are."

Analytical Dualism

A key element in the critical realist account of culture is the distinction between the cultural system and sociocultural interaction. The cultural system is the body of ideas and knowledge available to a society at a given time. Although the cultural system is a single system that encompasses all the ideas and knowledge available to a group, there may be contradictions within the system; the cultural system provides people with conflicting ideas and beliefs upon which they can draw, such as theism and atheism, or differing views on human sexuality. The cultural system also changes over time as new ideas and new knowledge are developed and as old ideas and knowledge are lost to time.[21]

Sociocultural interaction, on the other hand, focuses on human action—what theologians would call moral agency—and refers to how people draw on the knowledge and ideas of the cultural system in their interactions with one another. This includes not just interpersonal relationships but also the formation of larger social groups and institutions and the relationships among these groups within the broader society. Sociocultural interaction includes everything from a conflict at the kitchen table about a daughter's career aspirations and her parents' expectations to the efforts of the Black Lives Matter movement.

Sociocultural interactions can be characterized by conflict or by social integration, depending on whether social groups are able to draw on ideas from the cultural system to promote their interests and contest the interests of other groups, or if dominant social groups are able to appeal to ideas from the cultural system in ways that reinforce their position in society.[22] Critical realism therefore offers an account of culture that avoids "the myth of cultural integration" by adequately articulating how internal contradictions and social conflict can exist within a discrete cultural group.

Having distinguished the cultural system from sociocultural interaction, Archer puts forward the notion of "analytical dualism" to explain the relationship between the two. The cultural system and sociocultural interaction influence one another in two distinct but interrelated causal relationships. Personal choices and the interactions between people and social groups (sociocultural interaction) are made possible and yet are also constrained by the set of ideas, beliefs, and knowledge available to them (the cultural system) at any given time. Most of the time most people act within the cultural system without challenging it. But the choices of persons within sociocultural interactions also can transform the cultural system by generating new ideas and new knowledge over time.[23] Any adequate account of culture must take both of these causal relationships into account. In terms more familiar to theologians, culture conditions moral agency, and moral agency can transform culture. Chapter 4 identifies a similar relation between social structures and human agency.

Critical realism therefore rejects any approach to culture that claims that the causal influence between culture and agency runs only one way. Archer is critical of what she calls the "downward conflation" characteristic of the functionalist sociology associated with Talcott Parsons and the structuralist anthropology of Claude Lévi-Strauss. These schools of thought are examples of what Archer calls "methodological collectivism"—that is, an attempt to explain the influence of the cultural system on sociocultural interaction without adequately explaining the role that the actions of persons and groups in sociocultural interaction plays in either reproducing or transforming the cultural system.[24] In theological terms, this view leaves little room for human freedom or agency.

Archer also rejects the "upward conflation" of methodological individualism, in which culture is explained entirely in terms of the behaviors or beliefs of individual actors. In theological terms, this view celebrates human freedom to such an extent that freedom is seen (erroneously) as almost unconstrained by culture. One example of methodological individualism is the symbolic interactionism first proposed by the American sociologist George Herbert Mead.[25] According to this theory, individuals construct meaning through their interactions with one another. Although this theory recognizes that individuals interpret the world through a shared set of symbolic expressions, it fails to treat culture as a discrete reality that conditions human behavior; rather, it looks only at individuals' interpretations of their actions and the world beyond themselves. A more radical example is the rational choice theory of mainstream economics and much of political science today, which proposes that individuals act according to a rational calculation of costs and benefits. What we perceive as culture is seen as only a complex set of norms that have developed over time through the accumulation of individual choices. Like other forms of methodological individualism, rational choice theory ignores how individual actors are shaped by a preexisting culture.[26]

The Ontological Reality of the Cultural System

Critical realist sociology insists that the cultural system is ontologically real; it is distinct from the ideas, knowledge, and values present in individuals' minds at any given time, even though it has causal impact only through the actions of those individuals. To illustrate this point, Archer associates the cultural system with libraries, the repositories of a society's knowledge and ideas, although one would have to interpret this in the broadest possible sense to include the internet and other repositories of media and information.[27] Ideas or knowledge present in these repositories make up part of the cultural system even if no one is thinking of them because they nonetheless are available for use at any given time. This may seem like a strange claim, especially for theologians, since culture is often understood as the shared meaning communicated through words and actions. But like structures, culture emerges from the actions of people and exists at a "higher" level. The cultural system exerts a causal impact on human interaction, but it exercises this causal power only through the restrictions and opportunities it provides to persons employing this or that part of its resources.[28] Culture is always mediated through human agency.

This emphasis on the ontological reality of the cultural system and its causal powers distinguishes critical realism from what Archer calls the "central conflationism" of sociologists like Zygmunt Bauman and Anthony Giddens. Like the critical realists, Bauman and Giddens recognize that the cultural system and sociocultural interactions are mutually conditioning, but both insist that this takes place through a single, indistinct process they call "praxis" or "social practice," respectively. Culture, in this view, exists *only* in the minds of the agents who are conditioned by it and who reproduce it. Archer argues that this form of conflationism is ultimately incoherent; if the causal relationship between the cultural system and sociocultural interaction goes both ways, then social theorists must give an adequate account of the ontological realities behind those two distinct causal relationships.[29]

Culture and Structure

One last important feature of critical realism's approach to culture is that, although it distinguishes culture and structure, it also recognizes that the two mutually condition each other. As I noted earlier, one of the important contributions of critical realism is to clearly distinguish social structures, those aspects of social life dependent on material resources, from culture, which corresponds to the world of ideas. This distinction, however, should not be taken to suggest a radical independence between the material and ideational aspects of social life, as if they have no influence on each other. Rather, critical realism proposes that culture and structures are themselves mutually conditioning; indeed, the proper distinction between the two systems and their mechanisms is necessary for understanding the relationship between them. For example, in chapter 6 of this volume, David Cloutier discusses how the relationship between social structures and culture has contributed to the problem of climate change and how a response to the climate crisis must involve the transformation of both.

The reciprocal relationship between structure and culture can take a number of forms. For one, social structures condition the ability of individuals or social groups to draw upon the cultural system. For example, widespread illiteracy restricts people's access to the ideas and knowledge available to a particular society while allowing the more elite social classes to draw on those ideas to pursue their interests. Similarly, disparities in access to computers and the internet create unequal access to knowledge and ideas. Second, material resources enable social groups to promote ideas important to them. For example, political candidates with wealth or wealthy backers have more access to TV time to promote their candidacies. Third, the cultural system provides social groups with conceptual tools to justify their material interests. Dominant classes can appeal to certain ideas found in the cultural system to justify their dominant position in society, as US slave owners claimed a biblical endorsement in the nineteenth century. Similarly, however, marginalized groups can appeal to ideas from the cultural system to argue for a change in social structures, as Martin Luther King Jr. called on basic American and Christian values in his campaign for civil rights. Archer points out that while there is always a reciprocal relationship between structures and culture, the influence of one may predominate over the other in a given situation. Yet which has more influence can never be presumed; it must be discovered through social analysis.[30]

By recognizing the reciprocal relationship between structure and culture, critical realism distinguishes itself from social theories that see the causal influence between the two going in only one direction. For example, most forms of Marxism see culture as part of the "superstructure" that springs from and reinforces the economic system, or "base"; even those versions of Marxism that give culture some autonomous influence typically claim that ultimately the economic system plays the determinative role over the course of society. Critical realism, by contrast, recognizes that culture—ideas—can play a distinct role in shaping society and individual moral agency without downplaying the importance of material and economic factors. Likewise, critical realism rejects idealist interpretations of society that examine the history and development of ideas while largely ignoring social conditions and disparities in material resources. It also differs from postmodern social theories that interpret struggles to determine cultural meaning in terms of power but that downplay the material disparities that shape these struggles. For critical realism, cultural analysis can never be separated from the sociological analysis of social structures.

Critical realism therefore offers a way of understanding culture that avoids the problems Kathryn Tanner identifies with the "modern" meaning of culture while improving her analysis by offering more precise insights into culture and how it affects and is affected by human agency.

CRITICAL REALISM, CULTURE, AND THEOLOGY

What can the critical realist approach to culture offer to theologians? Earlier in this chapter I describe three areas in which contemporary theology engages with the notion of culture: secularization and pluralism, the inculturation of Christian theology and practice, and the critique of unjust cultural systems and practices. Critical realism's approach to culture could enhance the reflections of theologians working in all three of these fields. I can offer only brief suggestions for further reflection here, pointing toward areas where critical realism and theological reflection could fruitfully engage one another.

Secularization and Pluralism

One of the most pressing problems of theology since at least the nineteenth century has been that of the place of Christianity in the increasingly secular and pluralistic cultures of the West. For centuries, Christianity provided the integrating vision for social life in Europe and later the Americas, but through the gradual process of secularization the Christian religion has become increasingly privatized, unbelief more common, and religious pluralism more pronounced.[31] Christians have responded to this changed situation in a variety of ways, ranging from an enthusiastic embrace of modernity to antimodern retrenchment or fundamentalism.

These ongoing debates about the place of Christianity in an increasingly secular and pluralistic society raise a host of questions, and a more adequate understanding of culture inspired by critical realism can make a significant contribution to these discussions. For example, in *Theories of Culture*, Tanner makes the case that much of the discussion on the Christian response to secularization has been hampered by the belief that cultures are unified, cohesive wholes rather than diverse and fluid. Theologians have rightly discerned that Christianity functions like a culture, providing a set of beliefs, values, and practices that shape daily life, but have then gone astray in concluding that this means Christianity provides a complete, coherent way of life. Christian practice has always existed in a hybrid relationship with the surrounding culture. Denying this fact forces Christians into the false threefold choices of accommodation, living as a "counterculture," or dreaming of the restoration of a "Christian culture." Tanner proposes that once we understand that cultures can admit diversity and fluidity within their boundaries, it makes more sense to think of Christianity operating in and through culture while existing in a hybrid or dialogical relationship with other aspects of a given culture.[32]

The critical realist approach to culture can help flesh out Tanner's claims. Critical realism might approach secularization in a way consonant with the views laid out by Charles Taylor in A *Secular Age*. Taylor argues that secularization represented a change in the "social imaginary," such that we have undergone "a move from a society where belief in God is unchallenged and indeed, unproblematic, to one in which it is understood to be one option among others, and frequently not the easiest to embrace."[33] In other words, the cultural system has been transformed to include a number of contradictory ideas and beliefs about God and the world. At the same time, as a result of secularization, believers and nonbelievers alike share a historically new, desacralized view of the world, what Taylor calls "the immanent frame."[34] Therefore, it is unrealistic for Christians to long for the restoration of the sort of Christian society that existed before secularization because now the pluralization of beliefs characteristic of secularization is a robust part of the cultural system. Likewise, Christians ought to move beyond the dichotomy of accommodation with secular culture and a countercultural pose. Christians and their secular counterparts draw upon the same culture in their daily lives, even if they draw upon different aspects of that shared culture. It is better, then, to understand Christianity's role in a secular society as a form of cultural contestation at the sociocultural level rather than as an alternative society or culture.

Inculturation

Critical realism's account of culture also has much to offer theological discussions of inculturation or contextualization, the adaption of the Gospel to the diverse cultures of the world. Up until the twentieth century, Christian missionary endeavors were plagued by the problem of treating elements of European culture as if they were essential to the Gospel itself. This problem was compounded by the fact that in many cases Christian evangelization was closely connected to Western imperialism, such that Christian churches were implicated in the imposition of alien cultures onto local populations by colonial political authorities. Inculturation in part represents an effort to dissociate Christianity from European cultures and adapt the faith in non-Western contexts. Although this includes efforts such as using local languages in the liturgy and catechesis and the adaptation of local music for worship, most theologians reflecting on the process of inculturation have recognized that it requires a deeper encounter with the local culture and its worldview, including those religious traditions that have shaped the local culture.

This process of inculturation poses a number of profound questions. For example, in the encounter with a local culture, is Christianity's primary task to serve as a countercultural critic of those aspects of the local culture that seem to run counter to the Gospel, or is it to affirm the ways God may already be present in the local culture's beliefs and practices?[35] Taking the former approach risks the danger of cultural imperialism or of alienating local Christians from their own culture. It also risks failing to recognize the wisdom already present in the local culture, wisdom from which Christians themselves might learn. The latter approach, however, risks the danger of failing to challenge aspects of the local culture that do not promote human flourishing or that are ultimately incompatible with Christian belief.

A second set of questions revolves around the relationship between Christianity and religious traditions that are already part of the local culture. Since all religions work in and through culture and profoundly shape a culture's beliefs and practices, how does this affect the process of adapting Christianity to the local culture? The process of inculturation must authentically engage the local culture, including its religious elements, without resorting to syncretism, or the dilution of Christian orthodoxy through the blending of Christianity with other religious traditions. Asian theologians have given particular attention to these questions, given that Asia is home to major non-Christian religions of ancient lineage.[36]

Critical realism does not pretend to offer answers to these fundamentally theological and ethical questions, but it can offer tools for understanding culture that can assist theologians in their efforts. For one, critical realism provides a helpful way to think about diversity and conflict within cultures. As I noted earlier, critical realism helps explain how there can be contradictions within the cultural system and conflicts over cultural values and beliefs among social groups at the level of sociocultural interaction. This means that when Christianity encounters a culture, it typically does not encounter a cohesive, unified way of life but rather a diverse and even contradictory set of beliefs and practices as well as a number of social groups pushing the culture in different directions. This has important implications, for example, concerning questions about whether Christianity's proper function is to affirm or critique the local culture. Second, critical realism provides a compelling account of how a culture changes over time. Although agents are conditioned by their cultural system, because of their free choices in sociocultural interaction, they also transform the culture through the development of new ideas, practices, and knowledge. This account of cultural change could prove helpful in understanding how the introduction of Christianity changes the cultural system of a society, how Christian social groups transform a culture through interaction with other groups, and so on.

Critique of Unjust Cultural Systems and Practices

A third area where critical realism's account of culture would prove useful to theology is the theological critique of unjust cultural systems and practices. I focus in particular on the work of liberation theologians because they have given the most sustained attention to the systemic dimension of culture. Still, liberation theologians have often used terms such as "structural sin" or "structures of sin" indiscriminately, regardless of whether they are referring to social structures or to culture. Critical realism more clearly distinguishes between social structures and culture, empha-sizing that the two operate through distinct, although similar, mechanisms. At the same time, by distinguishing social structures from the cultural system, critical real-ism makes it possible to think more precisely about the relationships between, for example, the economic system and the cultural system. I will provide two examples of how these insights would prove useful to liberation theology.

Latin American liberation theology emerged as a method for doing theology from the perspective of the poor, or, as Gustavo Gutiérrez put it, "the underside of history."[37] Liberation theologians insisted that we have to see ourselves as situated within history, which means we must engage in a structural analysis of society to understand the forces that condition us and that oppress the poor. They turned to Marxist analysis and dependency theory as tools for interpreting Latin America's place in the global economy and the economic forces oppressing the poor. As Latin American liberation theology developed, however, theologians recognized that the "preferential option for the poor" included not only the economically poor but also other oppressed groups such as women and indigenous peoples.[38] Analyses of these forms of oppression had a cultural element that was not present before, so libera-tion theologians began to appeal to a variety of forms of social analysis but lacked a coherent social theoretical perspective. By providing a set of analytical tools that distinguish structures from culture but also describe the complex ways the two inter-act with and condition one another, critical realism can prove useful for theologians who wish to examine, for example, the relationships between the economic system, culture, and gender in Latin America.

In the United States beginning in the late 1960s, black liberation theologians have offered a theological critique of racism and white supremacy and proposed a form of Christian praxis that works toward a more inclusive church and society. One of the most prominent contemporary Catholic black liberation theologians is Bryan Massingale, who has reflected on racism within the US Catholic Church and on what the Catholic response to racism in the United States ought to be. In his book *Racial Justice and the Catholic Church*, Massingale asserts that "racism is a *cultural* phenomenon, that is, a way of interpreting human color differences that pervades the collective convictions, conventions, and practices of American life."[39] He explains how both "blackness" and "whiteness" are cultural constructs that inscribe inequal-ity into the American cultural system while also affirming that "blackness" generates a positive sense of cultural identity and belonging.[40] Massingale clearly describes the economic injustices that have historically been imposed on African Americans and explains the economic advantages that go alongside white privilege.[41] Likewise, he claims that any form of "affirmative redress" in response to the wounds of racism must consider the "material harms" and "economic disadvantages" experienced by African Americans.[42] Nevertheless, he analyzes racism primarily in terms of culture, without offering a properly structural analysis of racism and its effects. Critical real-ism offers a way of thinking about racism in the United States that could clarify the relationship between its cultural and structural elements.

CONCLUSION

The twentieth century witnessed a renaissance in Christian theological reflection on culture as many theologians borrowed from anthropologists an understanding of culture as a system of beliefs, values, and practices that give meaning to daily life. Theologians have reflected on a number of issues where the notion of culture plays a central role. For one, theologians have considered the place of Christian faith in increasingly secular and pluralistic cultures. Second, they have explored the issue of inculturation or contextualization, the adaption of the Gospel to the diverse cultures of the world. And third, theologians, most notably liberation theologians, have offered critiques of unjust cultural systems and practices.

To engage most fruitfully with these theological issues requires a precise understanding of culture, and theologians have drawn on a number of different social scientific perspectives in their work. In this chapter I have attempted to show some of the contributions that critical realist sociology has to offer theologians in its understanding of culture. Critical realism explains the relationship between what it calls the cultural system and sociocultural interaction—that is, the relation between the repository of knowledge and ideas available to a society at a given time and the interactions among individuals and social groups who are shaped by and draw upon the knowledge and ideas available to them. Critical realism proposes that the cultural system and sociocultural interaction are mutually conditioning; in other words, the cultural system conditions agents by making available to them certain ideas but not others, and yet agents can shape the cultural system by generating new ideas and knowledge through their interactions with one another. Critical realism also helps explain how there can be diversity and conflict within a single culture, a significant improvement over many modern notions of culture that have proved influential with theologians. Finally, critical realism also clearly distinguishes culture from social structures but also explains how the two influence one another.

Whatever understanding of the human person and moral agency a theologian may employ, a more detailed account of what culture is and how culture influences and is influenced by beliefs and choices will deepen theological insight.

NOTES

1. J. Peter Pham, "Uniting Faith and Culture: Hans Urs von Balthasar," *Imaginative Conservative* (blog), accessed January 1, 2018, http://www.theimaginativeconservative.org/2016/03/timeless-essays-uniting-faith-and-culture-hans-urs-von-balthasar.html.
2. Bernard J. F. Lonergan, *Philosophy of God and Theology* (Philadelphia: Westminster Press, 1973), 22.
3. For a history of this modern notion of culture, see Kathryn Tanner, *Theories of Culture: A New Agenda for Theology* (Minneapolis: Fortress Press, 1997), 3–24.

4. Second Vatican Council, *Gaudium et spes* (1965), 53. http://www.vatican.va/archive /hist_councils/ii_vatican_council/documents/vat-ii_const_19651207_gaudium-et-spes _en.html.

5. Robert Tucci, "Part II, Chapter II: The Proper Development of Culture," in *Commentary on the Documents of Vatican II*, vol. 5, *Pastoral Constitution on the Church in the Modern World*, ed. Herbert Vorgrimler, trans. W. J. O'Hara (New York: Herder & Herder, 1969), 256.

6. Second Vatican Council, *Gaudium et spes*, 58.

7. Second Vatican Council, 58.

8. Second Vatican Council.

9. José Casanova, *Public Religions in the Modern World* (Chicago: University of Chicago Press, 1994).

10. Stephen B. Bevans, *Models of Contextual Theology*, rev. ed. (Maryknoll, NY: Orbis Books, 2002).

11. Mary Mee-Yin Yuen, "Doing Local Theologies in the Asian Context—Implications of Inculturation since the Second Vatican Council," *Hong Kong Journal of Catholic Studies* (2010): 125–27.

12. Tanner, *Theories of Culture*, 25–29.

13. Tanner, 38–58.

14. Margaret S. Archer, *Culture and Agency: The Place of Culture in Social Theory*, rev. ed. (New York: Cambridge University Press, 1996), 1–21.

15. Archer, 1.

16. Margaret S. Archer, *Realist Social Theory: The Morphogenetic Approach* (New York: Cambridge University Press, 1995), 175.

17. Archer, 175.

18. On intelligibilia, see Archer, 180.

19. Margaret S. Archer, *Structure Agency and the Internal Conversation* (New York: Cambridge University Press, 2003), 2.

20. Archer, 2.

21. Archer, *Culture and Agency*, 130–42.

22. Archer, 185–226.

23. Archer, *Realist Social Theory*, 165–94.

24. Archer, *Culture and Agency*, 46–57.

25. George Herbert Mead, *Mind, Self, & Society from the Perspective of a Social Behaviorist*, ed. Charles W. Morris (Chicago: University of Chicago Press, 1934).

26. Archer and a number of other sociologists address the problems with rational choice theory in Margaret S. Archer and Jonathan Q. Tritter, eds., *Rational Choice Theory: Resisting Colonization* (New York: Routledge, 2000).

27. Archer, *Realist Social Theory*, 179.

28. Archer, 172–83.

29. Archer, *Culture and Agency*, 72–96.

30. Archer, 281–87.

31. Two of the best accounts of the process of secularization are José Casanova's *Public Religions in the Modern World* and Charles Taylor's *A Secular Age* (Cambridge, MA: Belknap Press, 2007).

32. Tanner, *Theories of Culture*, 93–119.

33. Taylor, *Secular Age*, 3.
34. Taylor, 544.
35. Bevans considers these and related questions in *Models of Contextual Theology*, 54–69, 117–38.
36. See, for example, Peter C. Phan, *Being Religious Interreligiously: Asian Perspectives on Interfaith Dialogue* (Maryknoll, NY: Orbis, 2004).
37. Gustavo Gutiérrez, *The Power of the Poor in History*, trans. Robert R. Barr (Maryknoll, NY: Orbis Books, 1983), 171–86.
38. On women, see, for example, María Pilar Aquino, *Our Cry for Life: Feminist Theology from Latin America*, trans. Dinah Livingtone (Maryknoll, NY: Orbis Books, 1993); and Ivone Gebara, *Out of the Depths: Women's Experience of Evil and Salvation*, trans. Ann Patrick Ware (Minneapolis: Fortress Press, 2003). On indigenous peoples, see Diego Irarrázaval, *Inculturation: New Dawn of the Church in Latin America*, trans. Phillip Berryman (Maryknoll, NY: Orbis Books, 2000).
39. Bryan Massingale, *Racial Justice and the Catholic Church* (Maryknoll, NY: Orbis Books, 2010). Emphasis in original.
40. Massingale, 13–33.
41. Massingale, 33–41.
42. Massingale, 100–102.

CHAPTER 6

Critical Realism and Climate Change

David Cloutier

Climate change, Willis Jenkins argues, "involves dimensions of human action without precedent in our traditions and institutions of justice."[1] No one intends it, and yet it proceeds ever faster. Its scale, complexity, and time frames all surpass ordinary modes of individual and social problem-solving. Thus, it has been dubbed a "wicked" or even "superwicked" problem because, among other things, its solution is a one-shot operation, is time-limited, pits future possibilities against present realities, and must come from the very people causing the problem.[2] If ever there was a moral challenge requiring an effective combination of structural analysis and personal moral agency, this is it.

What can critical realism contribute? I begin by outlining three typical approaches to the problem, all of which are important but differ significantly in their agendas for personal and social action. I then suggest that critical realism offers at least two valuable insights into the interplay of agency and structure that clarify the way forward among these options.

THREE APPROACHES

The problem of climate change is well rehearsed elsewhere. In its most basic form, it arises from massive increases in human emissions of greenhouse gases, resulting from the "great acceleration" of an increasingly energy-intensive way of life and an increasing population.[3] The disruption of the atmospheric conditions present for all of human history—in evolutionary terms, a swift change—creates actual and potential effects for many natural systems. While the *exact* consequences are necessarily uncertain, a firm scientific consensus supports major global effects that cannot be stopped once they pass certain tipping points. Economist William Nordhaus likens the problem to a "climate casino," in which future outcomes are probabilistic but in which it is prudent to (a) recognize the tendencies involved in the games and (b) avoid above all the worst possible outcomes.[4] Addressing the problem requires both global cooperation and personal lifestyle change. As Pope Francis points out in summing up his call for international collaboration, "Many things have to change course, but it is we human beings above all who need to change."[5]

The need to change is clear, but the questions about how to change are more difficult. Two of the best Christian ethicists writing on climate change are Willis Jenkins and Michael Northcott. Jenkins uses climate change as the benchmark example for a new approach to religious ethics he calls "prophetic pragmatism." He develops a lengthy argument against what he calls the "cosmological temptation," an ethics that "criticizes visions of reality," in which "all the important work happens at the level of moral ontology."[6] Such an approach, he argues, has two significant drawbacks. It "abstracts ethics from concrete problems," which "limits the relevant range of interdisciplinary exchange."[7] And it "can underscore the impossibility of any cooperative action until agents adopt a more satisfactory worldview."[8] Yet many proposals in Christian environmental ethics follow this route.[9] Jenkins calls for a different approach.

In light of the desperate need for interdisciplinary approaches and for cooperation across cultures and religions, Christian ethics should eschew cosmology and depend on the generative creativity of actual collaborations in addressing the broad range of climate challenges. Thus, for Jenkins, "Christian social ethics *arises from* missional projects that bear and respond to the world's problems as their own."[10] It ought to work "from specific problems with the moral values resident in a community," using various cosmological views as "moral inheritances" from which they might "invent adaptive responses."[11] Cultures should use their materials not as foundations but like a "tool kit" to "invent new cultural competencies" to set the ethical terms for confronting larger-scale problems.[12]

Michael Northcott, like Jenkins, is deeply appreciative of the complexity of the problem of climate change and, like Jenkins, wants to recognize its inherently political character. Northcott is direct in his challenge to structures: "Global warming is the earth's judgment on the global market empire, and on the heedless consumption it fosters."[13] He, too, writes skeptically about the kinds of ecological theologies dependent on abstract cosmological claims.[14] Yet for Northcott, modern pluralistic politics is a principal part of the problem. The "refusal to recognize moral and ecological constraints" is a "legacy of the European Enlightenment and the modern struggle for emancipation from the authority of the Church, tradition, and faith, as well as from nature."[15] While the Christian tradition itself shares in this decline narrative by failing in various ways, it is nevertheless the case that "to be modern" is to affirm a separation of "nature and culture."[16] Most importantly, it is "to deny that the weather is political" because it is "to deny that there is a God who is the author of both nature and culture."[17] Thus, Christians must respond to this catastrophe in the only way that is faithful and practical: re-form story-based practical cultures that inhabit the planet in fundamentally different ways, with the recognition that climate change is in fact appropriately "apocalyptic": it expresses a radical judgment on a sinful empire of self-worship and unprecedented consumption. Northcott suggests that grassroots movements like Britain's transition towns as well as efforts to block extraction hold the most promise; he does not think Enlightenment-based strategies such as securing "rights" for nature or expecting nation-states to regulate consumption can work. His emphasis is a recovery of a certain kind of "ecological society" that cultivates "virtues . . . only possible in the context of stable relationships of nurture and care, and of stable communities which are oriented towards both moral and spiritual fulfillment."[18]

Any reader of Jenkins and Northcott will recognize that they share a skepticism about a third approach, the "standard response" of a global incrementalism exemplified by the structure of the 2015 Paris Accord. While the accord must be hailed as progress by anyone concerned about the planet, marking real cooperation, it nevertheless "represents the easy part" of the process, not least because "it relies upon voluntary pledges of sovereign states that do not currently add up to anything close" to the (generally accepted) goal of limiting overall warming to 1.5 to 2 degrees Celsius.[19] The pledges of the United States amounted to about a 25 percent reduction in emissions, based principally on underlying "invisible" regulation of the dirtiest electricity, the overall fuel economy of the auto fleet, and the like. However, the United States probably needs something more like a 70 percent reduction from current emission levels to be sustainable.[20] Pope Francis rightly notes that small actions matter because they "call forth the goodness of others" and change the overall tenor of the society.[21] It is nevertheless the case that the weakly incrementalist approach of the Paris Accord is insufficient to face the challenge. As Kevin O'Brien notes, the accord "was both a success and a failure."[22] It represented "the best we can do" within the political limitations of the present order. Yet in order to reach anything like the necessary goals, such an approach places hope in speculative technological developments that will somehow enable a massive switch to "clean energy" with minimal lifestyle change—an approach that entrenches rather than counters the "anthropological roots of the crisis" in the "technocratic paradigm."[23]

While each of the three approaches is adequate to make a low-hanging-fruit argument against coal-fired power plants, they are strongly contrasting in both what agents should do and what structures facilitate right and wrong directions when faced with the full scale of the problem. Moreover, even on consensus matters like coal plants, things get complicated fast. Christian social ethics necessarily raises competing concerns about the effects of even modest changes in the energy supply on already impoverished coal-dependent communities.[24]

CRITICAL REALISM

Critical realism can help. A pivotal unsolved problem in the three approaches above is *how* social structures and cultures affect agents and the possibilities for transformation.

All agree that climate change is a problem that is complex and structural, but each implies quite different accounts of how to grasp these structures. The incremental approach denies that there is any fundamental problem with the market-state system, and so the only social theory needed is about how to mobilize enough people to get policy passed. Jenkins prefers a loose social theory—critical of aspects of the existing dominant order but committed to a variety of approaches "from below." Northcott, meanwhile, has a robust social theory—a fundamental critique of the existing order and an insistence on a movement to something very different.

Critical realism provides an overarching metatheory that is not so much a critique of any of these approaches as a way of making each more concrete and linking the approaches together in a way that makes some of their insights complementary. For example, both Jenkins and Northcott, in different ways, are quite critical of the mainstream market-state approach, yet their reliance on anecdotes of small-scale actions of resistance can raise questions about their adequacy to confront the unquestionably large-scale necessities imposed by the nature of the problem of climate change. They are right to point to local communities, but they need conceptual resources to explain how these initiatives might link up with broader efforts.

In what follows, I point to two ways in which critical realism can help. The first is its detailed analysis of how both structures and agents work in concert to maintain the status quo or effect social change. In particular, critical realism offers a differentiated, stratified view of action that enables an account of how particular positioned agents are embedded in larger social systems susceptible to change in particular ways. The second resource is critical realism's analysis of culture, which allows us to make sense of how culture is both a reality apart from agents that is nevertheless subject to change through particular modes of reflection by agents.

Social Structure

As already outlined in prior chapters, particularly Daniel Finn's chapters 3 and 4, critical realism provides a particularly powerful means by which to make sense of the claims about structural causation without eliminating the freedom of agents. At its most basic level, critical realism suggests that moral agency always emerges within preexisting social positions in which "the relations between its components are internal and necessary ones."[25] To occupy the position of the customer of an electric utility is to be an agent in particular necessary relations to other agents—such as the vice president of the utility and the members of a state commission on utilities. Of course, the force of "necessary" here is not meant to suggest that these positions mean precisely the same thing in all eras and cultures. Structures change over time, as critical realism powerfully reminds us, and this change is caused by agents. That is, it is not caused by unpositioned agents—by some kind of mythical free persons exercising unrestrained mastery over their utility choices. Instead, the positions of the structure preexist any agent, and they are objective—real—in that they involve given relations of material interest. Critical realism emphasizes that there are no unpositioned agents and that agents cannot pre-choose the characteristics of the positions they take up. Nevertheless, this does not mean the agents are not free; it just means that their free choices are shaped by the restrictions, opportunities, and incentives they face within that social structure.

The complex interplay of agents' positions and their "degrees of freedom" in relationship to restrictions, enablements, and incentives can be illustrated by three brief examples, all of which are relevant to climate change. Shared public transit can significantly lessen the carbon emissions of any agent, and minimizing one's impact via transit commuting (or even carpooling) to a job can be very meaningful. But, objectively, agents do not get to design for themselves the existing material infrastructure connecting residences and jobs; they enter into a preexisting system of positions that materially favors individual transportation by car. The agent's choices in that position are influenced but not determined. Agents who might desire to minimize their impact face costs in seeking sustainability. The use of public transit often imposes costs of time and coordination compared to the use of a private vehicle. The attempt to minimize these trade-offs can be challenging because (especially in certain larger cities) transit-friendly living options with relatively short commutes are increasingly desirable and therefore impose a different positional trade-off regarding size and cost of housing. Yet it is not all cost; some modes of transit may be lengthy but afford an opportunity for productive work that is not possible when driving. Further, these incentives themselves may depend on the configuration of one's profession. Finally, transportation planners (another set of agents) must try to take these restrictions and enablements into account because an underutilized transit system can increase overall carbon emissions. All these interacting structures do not *require* agents to make environmentally problematic choices, but they do shape "the situations in which they find themselves," imposing trade-offs in relation to other personal "projects," such as raising and caring for a family.[26]

A second example involves work travel. As Dan Daly illustrates in chapter 8, professionals may have some freedom in choosing to attend distant events, but insofar as their fields are structured in a certain way, the choice to eschew such events can also be professionally costly. They enter into established systems of networking and information flow, but, again, their choice is not determined, for they may be willing to accept a lower pace of professional advancement and potentially take advantage of how less travel will allow them more time with their families.

Finally, a third example: agents overseeing complex institutions face these kinds of trade-offs as they manage the collective footprint of their operations. For example, many colleges have entered a climate compact to achieve zero net emissions by 2050. My wealthy undergraduate institution is unusually committed on environmental issues. Yet a careful inventory of the institution's impact over time shows that, despite initiating many measures to improve sustainability, including two industrial-grade wind turbines, the average per-student carbon emissions have *risen* 25 percent in the two decades since I attended. Why? Because, the report suggests, of the proliferation of new buildings and new devices, both of which are necessary in the school's attempt to maintain its prestige level as an elite school. Like many other businesses, colleges must compete with peers for "customers," and the expectations of customers increase as other schools implement various amenities. This does not force any particular institution to build or add anything in particular, but a climate-driven reluctance will impose costs.

Critical realism is helpful in analyzing these sorts of structural problems in two ways. First, it offers a language that allows us to name with some precision the actual structures facing agency. The more precise naming can at least allow us to differentiate between problems such as the ones above and other sorts of choices where the agent's freedom is notably less constrained—and where their moral agency can exercise more responsibility. For example, faced with a car commute, agents also face the choice of a particular vehicle, and their choice of vehicle may involve far fewer restrictions in making a good, sustainable choice. The same may be said for the professional facing leisure travel choices, compared to business travel. Further, this construal of agents in positions also suggests that agents must have the "project" of sustainability included in their interests for there to be any hard choices at all.

This points us toward another helpful aspect of critical realism's structural analysis: its broader account of the possibilities for structural social change versus social stasis.[27] Highlighting the various structural positions and personal choices involved in a problem can lead to an analysis of "second-order relations between them, some of which will be emergent properties."[28] This second-order level—the level critical realism calls "system"—is where compatibilities and incompatibilities emerge that constitute the crucial leverage points for larger-scale change because these second-order emergent properties "affect large segments of the population, if not the whole of it."[29]

What might this insight do for thinking about climate change? The obvious leverage point would be the relative cheapness of choosing higher-emission options in many of the scenarios. As described in chapter 4, our current "system" has emerged from various choices and exists "above" individuals, leaving many people in positions where they face steep costs for adopting low-carbon habits. People might think differently about relocating far from family if, for example, they did not count on inexpensive air travel. Such examples could be multiplied almost indefinitely. A carbon price would entail a significant changing of the options faced by individuals in many different positions. As Nordhaus argues, the sheer complexity of attempts to regulate lower-order choices makes things like item rebates, light bulb regulations, or bag fees difficult, ineffectual, and probably much more expensive in terms of carbon bang for the buck.[30] A carbon price forces a recalibration of costs and incentives (if, as is assumed, some kind of energy dividend was also instituted as an incentive) throughout the entire system, from the simplest positions to the largest institutions.

Culture

Still, one might wonder how to get such a system-wide recalibration if the current structure is so skewed. This is where the critical realist treatment of the role of culture becomes crucial. As Matthew Shadle mentions in chapter 5, critical realism analytically differentiates between structural and cultural variables but also insists on their reciprocal relationship. Archer calls the interaction between *structural* emergent properties and *cultural* emergent properties a "third-order emergent"—where incompatibilities could be particularly potent for prompting change.[31]

How do we best understand this potency? Recall the distinction that critical realism makes between structures and culture. Whereas structures involve objective positions with vested interests, cultures involve "intelligibilia"—let's call them "ideas"—which have "logical relations" to one another.[32] These logical relations constitute the objectivity of culture. Just as social positions present persons with incentives and disincentives regardless of the agents that fill them, so, too, ideas have logical relations regardless "of people noticing them."[33] But, again, like structural positions, "any form of cultural conditioning only exerts its effects on people and is only efficacious through people" who are reflective, "due to their own emergent properties of self-consciousness and self-monitoring."[34] Agents in material positions face trade-offs but not forced choices. Agents amid a cultural landscape face a range of ideational relations not of their own making, but they are not simply forced to think or believe them.

This agency is what Archer means by referring to agents as "reflexive." Agent reflexivity is a necessary component of social explanation. Archer points out a key limitation of simple explanations of cultural "conditioning": the fact that "people do not respond in uniform fashion under the same structured circumstances."[35] Tendencies or trends are nothing more than that, not only because there is an openness to social systems but "partly because a second causal power is necessarily at play, namely the personal power to reflect subjectively upon one's circumstances and to decide what to do in them or to do about them."[36] Such agency crucially involves the fact that encultured agents always have things we *particularly* care about—philosophers call them "second-order desires" and Archer refers to them as "projects." An agent's projects in part emerge from the cultural context. However, even then, the agent both selects from among a wide range of possible projects and adjusts these projects in ongoing ways in relation to various aspects of "contextual feasibility."[37]

Considering climate change, here we encounter a crucial emergent contradiction, where today's cultural and structural systems exhibit real tension: people today do in fact want a world for themselves and their children that is stewarded well. At the same time, many agents live in a society whose structures are formed by a cultural idea of competitive individualism that is strongly oriented toward consumption as the chief avenue to happiness—what Brad Gregory sums up as the "goods life."[38] They make everyday choices that are not sustainable, and they may even know it. Many of their life projects in work and family end up being embedded in the positions and institutions of consumer society and its incentives toward economic growth. Yet it would be naive to understand this merely as a mechanical problem of structures. From quite a different perspective from Brad Gregory, ecologist James Gustave Speth calls the growth imperative "the secular religion of advancing industrial societies."[39] The growth imperative is particularly problematic in how it treats the longer term. Lester Thurow notes that in advanced capitalism, "the social context of individual preference formation is completely absent," leading to a situation where "everyone has an incentive to be a free rider" because of the lack of "a set of social norms that offsets a natural human tendency to emphasize the short run."[40] Speth insists that market reforms and policy formation cannot solve the problem by themselves. What is needed is "a deep change in social values— away from ever-increasing material consumption and toward close community and personal relationships, social solidarity, and a strong connection to nature."[41]

When Speth quips, "we may say that the best things in life are free, but not many of us act that way," he sums up a tension not simply between structure and culture but a tension that exists objectively within culture itself.[42] He makes clear that there is a logical conflict between the idea of a clean and sustainable use of resources and the ideas permeating consumer society about the pursuit of happiness. According to critical realism, this represents an objective contradiction in the cultural system, but, as with structures, such ideas do not have causal force except through agents—who are usually, according to Archer, reflective in various ways about what they value.

Archer catalogs four sorts of agential reflexivity that are particularly valuable for analyzing how agents deal with tensions they encounter in structures and culture. Communicative reflexives have an internal conversation that tends to reproduce the voices surrounding them; they are the community builders. Autonomous reflexives, by contrast, "seize the situational logic of opportunity" presented to them to pursue goals of success as incentivized by the structures of society; they are the individualists.[43] Her third type, meta-reflexives, also seek to establish a path forward for themselves but do so with more "critical detachment" from the opportunities and situational logics presented to them by dominant structures.[44] Autonomous reflexives seek "independence" but accept the terms of the choices presented, whereas meta-reflexives are more likely to question the choices. Finally, "fractured reflexives" are unable to generate fully the internal conversation required for effective agency. Instead of an orientation to "what is to be done," their reflection was merely "expressive" and served not to guide action but to "intensify affect."[45] In a sense, this fourth sort of reflexivity is a *lack* of agency, with the result of various forms of passivity (e.g., gut feelings, indecision, drifting along) to structural and cultural forces, often to the agent's long-term detriment.[46]

Archer's profound concern about fractured reflexivity in our world resonates well with the problem of the environment. For many people, an honest look at their lives will lead them into a recognition of the contradictions between the idea of good ecological stewardship and the idea of consumer-led growth via ever-better lifestyles. Some try to ignore or dissolve these contradictions to avoid the frustrated paralysis of fractured reflexivity. Climate change denial is a simple way to dissolve the contradiction, especially because (at least at a more detailed level) the science is somewhat difficult to understand. While some have argued that denial can be correlated with low overall scientific literacy, other studies suggest that certain underlying worldviews, formed mainly in terms of one's personal interests (or lack thereof) in business and commerce, are much more likely to correlate with such skepticism.[47] Another attempt to dissolve the problem: many environmentally concerned people, especially in business, adopt a naive technological optimism. The consumption regime can continue if we invent new technologies to consume more efficiently or to control the waste. Edward Parson of UCLA, and a consultant to the Obama White House on the environment, states that "you can understand climate change as a mostly technical problem to which there is a mostly technical solution."[48]

A further reason why agents tend to seek comfort in thin appeals to denial or technology is that while they value sustainability, they do not seem to value it very highly. Polls indicate most people in the United States do not believe that climate change will have much effect on their lives.[49] True, in some polls, an increasing number—nearly half—indicate that they "worry a great deal" about climate change and that it may "pose a serious threat in my lifetime."[50] However, these nonspecific poll questions do not get at the question of how such a concern might impinge on and force adjustment in personal projects. A 2016 poll interestingly found that a great majority of Americans were willing to pay an extra $1 a month on their electric bill to combat climate change, but support plummeted to 39 percent for a $10 charge and to 20 percent for a $50 charge. Of course, $50 a month is less than what many Americans pay for a couple's dinner out or cable TV service—and the survey did not ask an even more challenging set of questions about willingness to adopt lifestyle changes.[51] These findings suggest that while climate change may be a concern in the abstract, it often does not shape agency because it is not clearly connected to personal projects.

What is required to get past these challenges? Archer's category of meta-reflexivity is insightful because what is needed is a new sense of how one's *positive* personal projects might be more realizable in a lower-carbon-emission world. Such a world would likely be slower-paced, for example, something that is often expressed as desirable by many. Such an approach questions the standard choices on offer by the culture, being critical not only of key aspects of projects of the immediate past (e.g., giving up on suburban and exurban lifestyles) but also of the current present (e.g., questioning the fashionable cosmopolitan interest in travel) in favor of other projects (e.g., biking) that present possibilities for combining agential satisfaction and sustainability. This observation can be said to agree with both Jenkins and Northcott in particular ways. Like Jenkins, this meta-reflexivity that moves beyond the cultural contradictions into a new configuration may happen in multiple ways and need not rely on some wholesale change in cosmology. However, like Northcott, such meta-reflexivity recognizes and responds to an insight that a society with sustainable energy consumption practices is quite different from the one we've been used to for many decades.

OUR RESPONSE

Meta-reflexivity is descriptive of the sort of agency needed to deal with the cultural conflict between ideas of sustainability and of consumerism. Yet the extent of the challenge climate change poses means that Archer's category of fractured reflexivity appears relevant even for those who otherwise seem to be meta-reflexives on this issue. It is a familiar experience to hear the tinge of despair in an environmentalist's voice as they describe their inability to act in accord with their beliefs. In the introduction to his recent book on climate change, Kevin O'Brien notes, "I drive a car most days, I fly on planes a half-dozen times a year, and I eat food shipped from around the world." He even writes his words on a "computer with both a smartphone and tablet nearby"—and "these are just a few of the examples" from his lifestyle. He then goes on to argue that climate change must be understood as "violence" and "that I am guilty of this violence." He writes the book for those "who want to do something about it," but, while his confession is admirable, one cannot help but wonder what exactly he is doing as an agent.[52]

Of course, part of what critical realism can do here is bring more precision to the problem of positions and institutions—of structure—that O'Brien rightly recognizes is key. But critical realism also points to the limits of protests about structural problems; they are inadequate if people suffer from fractured reflexivity, in which they are not able to exercise effective agency, even when they possess considerable economic and professional privilege. Instead of agential action against violence, we get "intensified affect." Having been in a position similar to O'Brien, I wonder if maybe he could ditch the smartphone, carpool to work, and combine trips for travel to minimize back-and-forth flying. There are costs associated with all these possibilities, and things could structurally be done to shift those costs. However, the other half of the challenge is bringing a sense of joy and zeal to changing the basics of our lives in ways that are better for the planet. O'Brien's book rightly notes that climate change can be understood as a problem of violence; but surely if that's true, then the urgent imperative to change our direct actions, even if we pay some costs for doing so, is all the stronger. If even academics deeply concerned with climate change get stuck at lament, imagine the problem of fractured reflexivity faced by so many others with so much less privilege than ourselves.

The recognition of fractured reflexivity on this issue—and not just for "others" (e.g., coal miners, oil company executives, SUV drivers)—should certainly push us even more urgently to address structural facets of the problem. Yet some candor about what will have to change for agents personally is also necessary. "Living sustainably" just does not rank high enough in cases where seemingly more significant personal projects require unsustainable resource use. And this is true for very many of those in advanced countries. Thus, even while things like a smarter electrical grid and more renewable energy and better carbon taxation will help, the outcome is likely to be that the privileged (the upper-middle class) will financially be able to take advantage of a high-energy lifestyle, while that lifestyle will be priced out of reach for many middle-class families. This is neither politically palatable nor morally just.

As an alternative, privileged meta-reflexives ought to change aspects of our personal projects that are incompatible with sustainability because we are often the ones with more freedom to do so. A striking feature of many of Archer's interviews in

Making Our Way through the World is that meta-reflexives for whom religious faith (or, more broadly, helping others) grounded a profound sense of overarching vocation were often willing to make choices to pursue their vocational projects even when faced with paying significant costs. Many endured expensive educational detours, job uncertainty, familial stress, and long hours to realize their commitments. Christian ethicists, in particular, might consider how "helping the planet" could be seen as just as central to one's religious identity as love of neighbor—indeed, this is a central thrust of Pope Francis's *Laudato si'*. We also might consider how agents have adopted comparable personal commitments, such as vegetarianism, that require costs in daily life. How have agents come to recognize this as sufficiently important to their personal projects to pay those costs?

CONCLUSION

Providing analytical clarity about social structures and cultural ideas, critical realism offers Christian ethicists a template to understand the macrolevel factors that shape agency but also the dynamics of agents amid those macro factors. For the problem of climate change, this may make the problems seem more overwhelming. But I would suggest that these insights can allow Christian ethics to use its resources more effectively, in two ways. First, it provides specificity to the basic template of *Laudato si'* that our response must be both personal and social, both spiritual and political. That template is correct, but Christian ethicists should not stop at this vague, abstract level. Rather, we must develop normatively grounded accounts of the agency-structure relationships and better resources for the development of agent reflexivity that empowers action for change. In *Walking God's Earth*, I emphasize the need to go beyond a "list of environmental no-no's" and examine the most important broad patterns of our ordinary lives in relation to the use of natural resources, and I also seek to use deep theological resources from the Christian tradition (especially from Pope Benedict) to help people with a commitment to their Christian faith realize that the environment should be central to that commitment.[53] With critical realism, we are even better positioned to attend to *both* of these urgent tasks.

However, critical realism is not just a precision tool for analyzing issues; it is a reason for hope. It helps us realize how large-scale social changes can and do happen. They are not merely the product of grassroots improvisations or intentional vanguard communities (even if both of these play vital roles). As Archer puts it, "at the macroscopic level, it is the *relationship* between the structural system (materially grounded) and the cultural system (ideationally grounded)" that influences whether the overall social order is stable and reenacted by agents or whether it is transformed into something new.[54] Thus, if people come to *want* a different sort of society in their personal projects but are stuck with structures that still encourage the status quo, there is a fertile field for the possibility of change. A different example: a tension between increasing global structural incentives for clean energy (which are real[55]) and American cultural patterns still pining for a past order signal an objective conflict that opens doors of change via autonomous reflexives motivated by maintaining America's economic competitiveness.[56] It is these sorts of disjunctions in the social order that critical realism helps us pinpoint as sites where social change can occur.

But perhaps most importantly for Christian ethicists, critical realism reminds us that metaphors like "fertile fields" and "open doors" and "sites" still require agents to sow seeds or cross the threshold. Society is not a natural order. It is a social order of agents, and whether or not such changes occur will ultimately be determined by what agents do with the existing and emerging structural and ideational realities. Critical realism helps Christian ethics identify these structural realities but also gives us concrete reasons for Christians to be "doers of the word" and not just hearers.

NOTES

1. Willis Jenkins, *The Future of Ethics* (Washington, DC: Georgetown University Press, 2013), 1.
2. On wicked problems, see Horst Rittel and Melvin Webber, "Dilemmas in a General Theory of Planning," *Policy Sciences* 4 (1973): 155–69; and Kelly Levin, Benjamin Cashore, Steven Bernstein, and Graeme Auld, "Overcoming the Tragedy of Super Wicked Problems: Constraining Our Future Selves to Ameliorate Global Climate Change," *Policy Sciences* 45 (2012): 123–52.
3. J. R. McNeill and Peter Engelke, *The Great Acceleration: An Environmental History of the Anthropocene since 1945* (Cambridge, MA: Harvard University Press, 2014).
4. William D. Nordhaus, *Climate Casino: Risk, Uncertainty, and Economics for a Warming World* (New Haven, CT: Yale University Press, 2013).
5. Pope Francis, *Laudato si'*, no. 202, May 24, 2015.
6. Jenkins, *Future of Ethics*, 76–77.
7. Jenkins, 77.
8. Jenkins, 79.
9. Perhaps due in part to Lynn White's well-known critique of Christianity as causing the environmental crisis through its cosmology that desacralized nature and focused on an afterlife. Lynn White, "The Historical Roots of Our Ecologic Crisis," *Science* 155, no. 3767 (March 10, 1967): 1203–7; doi:10.1126/science.155.3767.1203.
10. Jenkins, *Future of Ethics*, 72. Italics added.
11. Jenkins, 168.
12. Jenkins, 171–72. Jenkins uses the example of a collaboration of environmentalists and conservatives in dealing with a sinking island in the bay; unfortunately, as is clear from this article, the island supported Donald Trump 87 percent, and its mayor argued against sea-level rise on national TV: AP, "Pro-Trump Mayor of Sinking Island Questions Al Gore on CNN," August 1, 2017; https://www.apnews.com/05dc8ec6fc3543 fba1c55cbaaab068c8.
13. Michael S. Northcott, *A Moral Climate: The Ethics of Global Warming* (Maryknoll, NY: Orbis Books, 2007), 7.

14. See Michael S. Northcott, *The Environment and Christian Ethics* (New York: Cambridge University Press, 1996), 161–63.
15. Northcott, *Moral Climate*, 6.
16. Michael S. Northcott, *A Political Theology of Climate Change* (Grand Rapids, MI: Eerdmans, 2013), 44–45.
17. Northcott, *Political Theology of Climate Change*, 46.
18. Northcott, *Environment and Christian Ethics*, 316.
19. Laurence C. Smith, "Greenhouse Warning: Prepare for the Worst," *New York Review of Books* (October 13, 2016), 44.
20. This estimate comes from Tim Flannery, *The Weather Makers* (New York: Grove Press, 2006), 303. Other estimates of the scale of change required by the highest-emitting economies are even higher.
21. Pope Francis, *Laudato si'*, no. 212.
22. Kevin J. O'Brien, *The Violence of Climate Change: Lessons of Resistance from Nonviolence Activists* (Washington, DC: Georgetown University Press, 2017), 18.
23. Pope Francis, *Laudato si'*, nos. 101–14.
24. See, for example, Anne Clifford, "The Significance of Pope Francis's Prophetic Call: 'Care for Our Common Home' for Northern Appalachia," *Journal of Moral Theology* 6, special issue no. 1 (2017): 1–21, as well as other essays in this number of the journal, focused on the region.
25. Margaret S. Archer, *Realist Social Theory: A Morphogenetic Approach* (New York: Cambridge University Press, 1995), 172–73.
26. Archer, *Realist Social Theory*, 196.
27. Archer calls change "morphogenesis" and reinforcement of existing structures "morphostasis."
28. Archer, *Realist Social Theory*, 188–89.
29. Archer, 213–15.
30. Nordhaus, *Climate Casino*, 263–64.
31. Archer, *Realist Social Theory*, 218.
32. Archer, 180.
33. Archer, 181.
34. Archer, 184.
35. Margaret S. Archer, *Making Our Way through the World: Human Reflexivity and Social Mobility* (Cambridge: Cambridge University Press, 2007), 11.
36. Archer, 11.
37. Archer, 21–22. Historically, Archer contends that no society would be possible without some reflexivity, and so she rejects myths that traditional societies did not involve any "sense of self." But she does suggest that contemporary societies have generally expanded the "scope and range" of reflexivity. Archer, 25–29.
38. Brad Gregory, *The Unintended Reformation: How a Religious Revolution Secularized Society* (Cambridge, MA: Belknap Press, 2012).
39. James Gustave Speth, *The Bridge at the Edge of the World: Capitalism, the Environment, and Crossing from Crisis to Sustainability* (New Haven, CT: Yale University Press, 2008), 47.
40. Lester Thurow, *The Future of Capitalism: How Today's Economic Forces Will Shape Tomorrow's Future* (New York: William Morrow, 1996), 297–306.
41. Thurow, 44.
42. Speth, *The Bridge*, 67.

43. Interestingly, their backgrounds, Archer reports, "reflected the absence of relational goods rather than the presence of relational evils." See Margaret S. Archer, *The Reflexive Imperative in Late Modernity* (New York: Cambridge University Press, 2012).
44. Archer, 210.
45. Archer, 251.
46. Archer, 252.
47. On low overall scientific literacy, see Nick Pidgeon and Baruch Fischoff, "The Role of Social and Decision Sciences in Communicating Uncertain Climate Risks," *Nature Climate Change* 1, no. 1 (2011): 35–41; and C. R. Sunstein, "On the Divergent American Reactions to Terrorism and Climate Change," *Columbia Law Review*, no. 107 (2007): 503–57. On worldviews, see Dan M. Kahan, Ellen Peters, Maggie Wittlin, Paul Slovic, Lisa Larrimore Ouellette, Donald Braman, and Gregory Mandel, "The Polarizing Impact of Science Literacy and Numeracy on Perceived Climate Change Risks," *Nature Climate Change* 2 (2012): 732–35. For more, see also James Gilden and Ellen Peters, "Public Knowledge, Scientific Literacy, Numeracy, and Perceptions of Climate Change," April 2017, http://climatescience.oxfordre.com/view/10.1093/acrefore/978019 0228620.001.0001/acrefore-9780190228620-e-305.
48. Quoted in Damon Beres, "Can Tech Stop Climate Change? We Asked an Expert," *Huffington Post*, December 14, 2015, http://www.huffingtonpost.com/entry/tech-climate -change_us_566f2719e4b0fccee16f7215. Unsurprisingly, Parson advocates strongly for new and better nuclear fuel, with technological enhancements that will make long-term storage safe.
49. Nadja Popovich, John Schwartz, and Tatiana Schlossberg, "How Americans Think about Climate Change in Six Maps," *New York Times*, March 21, 2017, https://www.nytimes .com/interactive/2017/03/21/climate/how-americans-think-about-climate-change-in-six -maps.html?_r=0.
50. Lydia Saad, "Global Warming Concern at Three Decade High in U.S.," *Gallup News*, March 14, 2017, http://www.gallup.com/poll/206030/global-warming-concern-three -decade-high.aspx.
51. "Americans Willing to Pay to Fight Climate Change (but Only a Little)," Associated Press, September 15, 2016, http://www.cbsnews.com/news/americans-money-to-fight -global-warming-climate-change/.
52. O'Brien, *Violence of Climate Change*, 3.
53. David Cloutier, *Walking God's Earth: The Environment and Catholic Faith* (Collegeville, MN: Liturgical Press, 2014).
54. Archer, *Making Our Way*, 49.
55. See, for example, a recent, very clear article from climate researchers: Christiana Figueres, Hans Joachim Schellnhuber, Gail Whiteman, Johan Rockström, Anthony Hobley, and Stefan Rahmstorf, "Three Years to Safeguard Our Climate," *Nature*, no. 546 (June 29, 2017): 593–95, https://www.nature.com/news/three-years-to-safeguard -our-climate-1.22201.
56. One could also mention the extent to which the American military recognizes how climate change will likely bring tremendous instability and possibilities of violence around the globe. If sustainability and national security can be aligned, such that changing our energy habits is a matter of patriotic duty, many more agents will integrate it into their personal projects.

CHAPTER 7

Critical Realism and the Economy

Matthew A. Shadle

People of faith today strive to live out a morally responsible life in a world with problems of immense breadth and depth—from global threats of climate change to the interior emptiness of consumer culture. The contours of economic life become ever more intrusive in daily activities as the news informs us more frequently about the stock market than the weather and economic insecurity weighs on more and more people.

From the earliest centuries of Christianity, ethical reflection has addressed not only interpersonal issues of morality but social, political, and economic life as well. In the modern era, the Catholic Church has offered guidance on the rights of workers, on how to structure national economic life for the sake of the common good, and on authentic development in the Global South. In doing so, the Church's social teaching has benefited from the experience of economic life in diverse nations and from a variety of schools of economic thought. Today critical realism offers a set of analytical tools that can enrich the Church's social teaching and help it address the problems faced in our global capitalist economy, both through its understanding of moral agency within social structures and through institutional economics, an economic school of thought recently influenced by critical realism.

In this chapter, I explore how critical realism offers a method that complements the vision of the person in community that guides the Church's economic teaching. I also show how critical realism and institutional economics can enrich the Church's claim to present an alternative to the extremes of capitalism and socialism in its social teaching and point toward new directions for the Church's thinking about economic life. Although the focus here is on Catholic social teaching, much of what follows can be helpful to Christian ethics more generally.

CATHOLIC SOCIAL TEACHING
AND ECONOMIC THOUGHT

Modern Catholic social teaching began as a response to the rapid and profound changes to economic life brought about by the Industrial Revolution and the subsequent spread of capitalism. Pope Leo XIII published his encyclical *Rerum novarum* in 1891 to voice support for the rights of workers to earn a fair wage and to form unions but also to defend the right to private property against the socialist movements that were gaining steam at the end of the nineteenth century. Leo's encyclical built on the work of a number of Catholics throughout Europe who had helped workers organize into associations to better advocate for their rights and had worked for legislative reforms to ameliorate conditions in the workplace.[1] Even as official Catholic social teaching expanded to include other issues in the decades that followed, the economy continued to be a central focus. In the past fifty years that focus has broadened to encompass development in the Global South with Pope Paul VI's 1967 encyclical *Populorum progressio* and the phenomenon of globalization in Pope Benedict XVI's 2009 encyclical *Caritas in veritate*.

Throughout its long history, Catholic social teaching has positioned itself as an alternative to the dominant economic ideologies of capitalist individualism and socialist collectivism. In *Rerum novarum* Pope Leo challenged both the capitalism and the socialism of his day, and by the time of Pope Pius XI's 1931 encyclical *Quadragesimo anno*, it was common to claim that Catholic social teaching offered a "Third Way" between capitalism of the West and the communism of the USSR. After the Second World War, Christian democratic political parties in Western Europe drew on Catholic social teaching to offer a "social capitalist" economic alternative.[2] In Latin America, Christian democrats of the 1960s advocated sweeping economic reforms that challenged the capitalist status quo but offered an alternative to the Marxist revolutionary movements then gaining support.

With the end of the Cold War and the emergence of a more integrated, global capitalist economy, Catholic social teaching has come to more clearly acknowledge the positive aspects of the market but has also remained harshly critical of the consumerism, environmental degradation, and exploitation of the poor so common in global markets. In particular, popes John Paul II, Benedict XVI, and Francis have censured the effects of neoliberal globalization on the poor and on developing nations of the Global South, joining a chorus of secular critics. The financial crisis of 2007–8 led more people to search for an alternative to liberal capitalism, aiming for a new and more humane form of economic life. Given its history of seeking an economic system that is neither free market capitalism nor centrally planned socialism, Catholic social teaching has much to contribute to this quest. Yet the spread of capitalism around the globe is matched by the hegemony of neoclassical economics within the academy and policy think tanks. To strengthen its effectiveness, Catholic social teaching must find a way to challenge not only the injustices of the present economic system but also that system's intellectual underpinnings.

It is the purpose of this volume to argue that critical realism has an extraordinary contribution to make to enrich Christian teaching on economic life. Critical realism offers an understanding of the relationship between the moral agency of individuals and the causal influence of social structures that can strengthen Catholic social teaching's communitarian vision of the economy. In addition, the school of institutional economics proposes a method for studying the economy that draws on critical realist social theory and provides an alternative to the hegemony of neoclassical economics. Institutional economics rejects the notion central to mainstream economics that the individual economic agent is a rational actor whose preferences are "given" and instead proposes that the individual's interests are shaped by the economic institutions and broader social context in which they act. It also studies the economy in structural terms, describing it as a complex system of institutions that evolves over time. Although contemporary institutional economics draws on a number of intellectual sources, two of its leading practitioners, Geoffrey M. Hodgson and Tony Lawson, explicitly appeal to critical realism as a theoretical foundation for their work. In the next section, I explore how critical realism and institutional economics provide a methodological approach to the economy that complements Catholic social teaching's ontological and normative claims about the individual and community and its claim to offer an alternative to the extremes of capitalism and socialism. In the last section, I show how institutional economics' vision of the economy can contribute insights into long-standing debates over the economy within Christian circles.

PERSONS IN COMMUNITY: BEYOND INDIVIDUALISM AND COLLECTIVISM

The Second Vatican Council's "Pastoral Constitution on the Church in the Modern World," *Gaudium et spes*, offers a concise summary of what could be called the Catholic vision of the person in community. The document's first chapter describes the human person as a unity of body and soul possessed of both intellect and free will. The human person bears inviolable dignity because he or she is created in the image of God and is called to communion with God.[3] The next chapter emphasizes what it calls the "social nature" of humankind.[4] Human persons live in community because they are interdependent. Together human communities are called to work toward the common good.[5] *Gaudium et spes* is clear, however, that the pursuit of the common good does not entail sacrificing the individual in a form of collectivism but rather "the subject and the goal of all social institutions is and must be the human person which for its part and by its very nature stands completely in need of social life."[6] This Catholic vision of the person in community therefore rejects any form of individualism or collectivism, seeing instead a reciprocal relationship between the individual and the community.

This vision of the person in community provides the foundation for more particular tenets concerning the economy. For example, Catholic social teaching defends the right to private property as an instrument for the freedom and creativity of the person but also insists on what it calls the "universal destination of goods"— that is, the moral responsibility to use and share one's wealth in ways that promote the well-being of everyone. It also proposes that the owners of business enterprises should provide workers with a share in the management, or even ownership, of the company and recommends the establishment of cooperative enterprises in which the workers themselves are joint owners. The business enterprise ought to be a true community of persons.[7] Catholic social teaching also insists that each person is the bearer of certain economic rights such as the rights to food, adequate health care, and a just wage as a consequence of the human dignity he or she possesses. Such economic needs are to be met through a combination of personal economic initiative and the efforts of both civil society and the state, all working toward the common good.

This ontological and normative vision of the person in community has provided inspiration for Catholics over many decades and across multiple continents. Critical realism supplements these claims with a methodological approach to social theory that likewise finds a reciprocal relationship between the individual and the community, or what in sociology are termed agency and structure. Critical realism proposes that agents and structures are mutually constitutive. That is, each plays a role in shaping the other. On the one hand, social structures enable and constrain individual agents by distributing material resources among them and positioning agents in relation to one another concerning factors such as race, class, or gender. On the other hand, agents either support structures (when making decisions in accord with the restrictions and opportunities they face) or challenge them (when they resist those forces). For example, by transforming structures, resources can be redistributed or the positions of social groups can shift relative to one another.[8]

As explained in more detail in chapter 4, this approach to understanding the relationship between agents and structure departs from the two previously dominant approaches to social theory: methodological individualism and methodological holism. Methodological individualism attempts to explain social life solely in terms of the behavior of individual agents and denies the reality of social structures that have an independent causal influence on the behavior of individuals.[9] Methodological holism, meanwhile, interprets individual behavior as the product of social forces and allows for very little if any autonomous causality (i.e., freedom) on the part of the individual agent.[10] Sociologist Margaret Archer is also careful to distinguish critical realism from the structuration theory of Anthony Giddens. Like critical realism, structuration theory sees agents and structures as mutually constitutive, but it interprets this reciprocal relationship as a single, ongoing process. Archer argues that Giddens fails to distinguish between the causal impact that structures have on agents, on the one hand, and that agents have on structures, on the other. She is clear that making this distinction involves an ontological claim that both agents and social structures are distinct, real entities with independent causal power (hence critical *realism*). She labels this approach "analytical dualism," emphasizing the duality of agency and structure as well as the two distinct causal relationships between them.[11]

As Geoffrey Hodgson explains, institutions and social systems exist, in a sense, between agents and structures. A system is a broad, organized pattern of behavior conditioned by both culture and structure: the economy, the political system, the educational system, and so on. Institutions are the most fundamental elements of a system, and in the capitalist economic system, they include money, the business firm, property rights, banks, and so on. Institutions are reproduced and transformed through the interaction of agents, but they also take on structural features, conditioning the identities and behaviors of agents.[12]

Archer rightly recognizes that any sociological methodology entails an underlying ontology. Critical realism proposes an ontology in which both individuals and social structures are real entities. Individuals are linked to one another through the structures and institutions they share, and those structures and institutions condition and shape individuals' decisions and identities. Individual persons are not entirely the products of society; they act with autonomous agency (moral freedom in theological terms) and decide how they respond to the constraints and opportunities facing them. This social ontology has much in common with that found in Catholic teaching, outlined above. For this reason, critical realism provides a powerful tool for enriching and deepening Catholic social teaching's normative claims about the economy since the latter is founded upon Catholicism's ontology of the person in community. As I noted earlier, Catholicism's communitarian vision of society has long been viewed as an alternative to both individualism and collectivism, and its economic teaching as an alternative to both laissez-faire capitalism and centrally planned socialism. In the next section, I explain how critical realism and institutional economics, which draws inspiration from critical realism, offer critiques of both mainstream economics and Marxism. I also show how these relate to the critiques of capitalism and socialism leveled by Catholic social teaching.

THE CRITIQUE OF FREE MARKET ECONOMICS

One of the hallmarks of mainstream economics is the belief that individuals are rational "maximizing" actors who make choices based on their self-interest. Most economists would agree that this so-called *homo economicus* is not an accurate portrayal of actual human behavior but that it still provides a useful model that helps make economic predictions.[13] Indeed, the construct of *homo economicus* is the foundation of microeconomic descriptions of the behavior of individual consumers and firms, and indirectly of the aggregate phenomena studied by macroeconomics. A primary aspect of this vision of the economic agent is that the person's interests are *exogenous* to the system. That is, the person's wants or desires are not influenced by the economic system itself but rather come from elsewhere and exist prior to the individual's entry into the economic system. The individual agent's sense of what is best for him is thereby exogenous to the system and not to be questioned. Of course, in this view, the decisions of individuals and firms are shaped by the conditions of the market, such as the relative market position of competing firms or the price of particular products, but the goals of rational action (understood as a utility calculation) brought to the decision are characteristics of the individual actor uninfluenced by surrounding conditions. The subfield of economics known as behavioral economics has explored how economic actors often behave in irrational ways due, for example, to psychological biases in perception, but it has not dissuaded most economists from a conviction that people are rational maximizers.

A second underlying presupposition of mainstream economics is that the institutions of the market are in a sense natural. As rational actors seeking their self-interest, individuals naturally engage in the exchange of goods and services in the market. A pithy expression of this belief comes from the Nobel Prize–winning economist Oliver Williamson, who states, "In the beginning there were markets."[14] This suggests that the market exchanges characteristic of capitalism come naturally to human beings and, at least at a basic level, have remain unchanged throughout human history. Of course, mainstream economists are aware that the institutions of the modern economy—the corporation, banking institutions, modern money—developed over time. They propose, however, that these institutions evolved through the accumulated actions of rational individuals; over time rational actors developed a set of rules to facilitate the pursuit of their self-interest, rules that became the capitalist system of today. A well-known example is the theory that people spontaneously developed the institution of money as a more rational way of carrying out market exchanges than was available through barter. These institutions are "natural," then, not in the sense that they are primordial but instead that they are a spontaneous outgrowth of rational economic behavior and facilitate market exchange between individuals.

Again, mainstream economists are aware that most societies throughout human history have not had free market economies. How, then, could the market economy be natural given its rarity throughout human history? Many mainstream economists suggest that over time market exchange has been distorted by noneconomic factors such as government interventions, cultural norms, and religious taboos. The emergence of modern capitalism therefore embodies the recognition that these distortions hinder the creation of wealth and that policies eliminating these distortions (to allow the market to operate freely) ought to be pursued.

As suggested by Williamson's claim that markets were around "in the beginning," there is a quasi-religious quality to mainstream claims that individuals are rational actors and that market institutions are natural. These claims provide a compelling narrative about how the economy works, but they do not stand up to scrutiny.

As Geoffrey Hodgson points out, the behaviors, moral norms, and rational calculations attributed to individuals can be explained only if the individual is already embedded in a network of social relations. Mainstream economists attempt to explain the emergence of market institutions as the result simply of the interaction of individuals over time, but the individual behaviors used to explain this process themselves are governed by a set of institutions, rules, and shared conventions that remain unacknowledged and unexplained within the discipline. For example, Hodgson notes that some explain the emergence of economic institutions as the result of individuals' preferences for cooperation or altruism without realizing that notions such as cooperation and altruism already presume a set of shared conventions or norms if they are to have any practical meaning.

Likewise, other mainstream economists appeal to game theory to show that after repeated instances of a simplified game, participants can develop a set of shared rules or conventions to maximize each individual's benefit. This is meant to show how free markets could have emerged naturally from individual decisions over time. Yet, Hodgson suggests, even the simplest scenario proposed by game theory (such as "the prisoner's dilemma") presupposes that the participants share an understanding of the "rules of the game." Where did these rules come from? Perhaps they developed through repeated instances of a different game, but then that game must have had its own rules. Either one is faced with an infinite regress or one must admit that society has causal power independent of individuals and that individual actors are conditioned by these social structures.[15]

As a result, the claim that market institutions represent a sort of natural state falls apart as well. Williamson's views on human origins to the contrary, markets did not develop spontaneously over time through the interaction of individuals. The historian and sociologist Karl Polanyi showed long ago that the emergence of modern capitalist institutions came about through deliberate political decisions, such as the enclosure of pasture lands and reform of poor laws in England, rather than through a spontaneous process.[16] Resonating with fundamental convictions of critical realist sociology, institutional economics proposes in addition that individual behaviors are always already conditioned by economic institutions and social conventions and that therefore no system of economic institutions is more natural than another. It is true that institutions often emerge, are maintained, or are transformed "spontaneously," in that most people most of the time do not deliberately set about creating, maintaining, or changing these institutions through their economic activity. However, the distinction between spontaneously emerging and deliberately planned institutions loses its salience once one admits that all behavior is socially conditioned.

This institutionalist and critical realist approach to the economy enriches Catholic social teaching's long-standing critiques of capitalism in a number of ways, but here I focus on two. First, Catholic social teaching insists on the universal destination of goods, the responsibility to use private property to help meet the needs of others and promote the common good. Institutional economics offers what might be called an ontology of property that complements this claim. Mainstream economists typically understand property ownership to be equivalent to possession—that is, the ability to control and use something, which is a relationship between an individual and an object. The legal institution of property is understood merely as a codification of this pre-social right meant to facilitate market exchange. But Hodgson argues that this is a misconception of the character of property, which is inherently social. The legal institution of property entails recognition by others, a process of transfer between owners, and a process of adjudication and enforcement when conflict arises, none of which are entailed by mere possession. Property ownership does not preexist society but rather is a creation of society.[17] This being the case, then, Catholic social teaching's claim that property ownership brings with it social obligations gains added force since property itself, although privately owned, is a *social* institution maintained and protected by society. Thomas Aquinas himself claimed that personal ownership of things was a human invention, a wise addition to the natural law, and the insights of institutional economics and critical realist sociology now articulate how that occurs in more detail.[18]

Consumerism presents a second example of how critical realism and institutional economics can enrich Catholic social teaching. When many Europeans and Americans began experiencing increasing material affluence after the Second World War, consumerism became a concern for Catholic social teaching. This was not because material prosperity is bad in itself, since it contributes to more humane living conditions, but rather because it creates the temptation to ignore spiritual values and one's responsibilities toward the common good.[19] The problem of consumerism became a major focus of concern in the teaching of John Paul II. In his 1987 encyclical *Sollicitudo rei socialis*, for example, he contrasts the consumerism rampant in the developed world with the poverty in the underdeveloped world, claiming that this imbalance arises when "having" is given priority over "being"—that is, when people focus on the accumulation of material things over the authentic development of themselves and others.[20] John Paul makes much the same point in his 1991 encyclical *Centesimus annus*.[21]

Catholic advocates for the free market, such as Michael Novak and Richard Neuhaus, have attempted to minimize concerns that market economies encourage consumerism. Neuhaus even goes so far as to call John Paul's treatment of the issue in *Centesimus annus* as a "throwaway line" that does not fit with the main thrust of the encyclical in favor of free markets.[22] In this view, the freedom of the free market enables people to make materialistic choices but also noble ones. Consumerism is primarily a matter of individual virtue or vice and represents a failure of the cultural sphere rather than of the economic sphere. John Paul II, however, does not interpret consumerism in such an individualistic way; in *Centesimus annus* he describes it as a "structure of sin" in the human environment.[23] Although he notes that his criticisms of consumerism "are directed not so much against an economic system as against an ethical and cultural system," this is not intended to *exclude* the economic system from critique but rather to point to the fact that the economic system is embedded within a larger cultural system.[24] As he writes elsewhere in the encyclical, "All human activity takes place within a culture and interacts with culture."[25] The contemporary capitalist economic system encourages consumerism because it embodies and perpetuates a consumerist culture.

Critical realism and institutional economics can provide insight into Pope John Paul II's claims. By insisting that consumerism is a structure of sin, John Paul is claiming that the phenomenon of consumerism cannot be reduced to a matter of individual choice or personal vices; there are social forces that exercise causal power in a way that shapes and conditions the behaviors and attitudes of individual consumers. In chapter 8 of this volume, Daniel Daly explores in more detail how personal virtues and vices such as consumerism necessarily have a structural element that critical realism can help elucidate. Critical realism also proposes that culture and structure condition individual agents in similar but distinct ways, as noted in chapter 5 of this volume. It suggests that culture and structures interact with each other and mutually condition each other.[26] Critical realism and institutional economics therefore offer valuable insights into the intersection between the culture of consumerism and the institutions of contemporary capitalism such as modern marketing and advertising and the dominance of the market by massive multinational corporations.[27]

THE CRITIQUE OF MARXISM

Whereas critical realism and institutional economics are critical of the methodological individualism employed by neoclassical economics, they challenge Marxism for its methodological holism. Critical realism and Marxism share the belief that individual agents are conditioned by social structures. As Marx wrote, "Men make their own history, but not . . . under circumstances they themselves have chosen but under the given and inherited circumstances with which they are directly confronted."[28] Yet in Marx's work, there is a tendency to see individual agents as entirely the product of social forces. For example, in the third volume of *Capital*, Marx writes that "the principal agents of this [capitalist] mode of production itself, the capitalist and the wage-labourer, are as such simply embodiments and personifications of capital and wage-labour—specific social characters that the social production process stamps on individuals, products of these specific social relations of production."[29] As Hodgson notes, although there is some nuance to Marx's thought, it clearly tilts toward a methodological holist perspective, a tendency that dominated later Marxist thought.[30]

One problem that Hodgson identifies with Marxism's holism is that, ironically, it fails to provide an account of *how* an individual is shaped and conditioned by social structures. Although it assumes that "the social relations of production" impress on individuals' particular beliefs or behaviors, it does not provide an adequate description of the mechanisms through which this takes place. As Hodgson argues, providing such an account would mean recognizing the ontological distinctiveness of the individual agent and therefore his or her causal power as distinct from that of social structures.[31] For example, Marx attempts such an explanation by proposing that the development of new technologies of production ultimately drives social transformation by changing the organization of production and the consciousness of workers.[32] A closer look at how workers interact with technology, however, would show that workers are not passively shaped by the technology they use but rather interact with it by drawing on a store of practical and technical knowledge gained through individual experience and learning from the community of workers.[33] Although technologies of production unquestionably impact the organization of economic life, workers are also agents who shape the production process.

In *Centesimus annus*, Pope John Paul II points out that the nations of the communist bloc, although in name dedicated to workers, ended up exploiting workers.[34] He had earlier explored the ultimate reasons for this exploitation in his 1981 encyclical *Laborem exercens*, where he distinguished between the objective and the subjective dimensions of work. The objective dimension of work refers to the worker's interaction with external objects, to technology and the methods of production.[35] The subjective dimension, on the other hand, refers to the fact that work is carried out by "a conscious and free subject."[36] Work is not just a technical procedure but a process of personal self-realization. John Paul goes on to argue that this subjective dimension of work has preeminence over the objective, a principle he refers to as the priority of labor over capital.[37]

John Paul uses this principle to interpret modern economic history. With early capitalism, the worker had come to be seen as merely a "factor of production," focusing on the objective dimension of work while ignoring the subjective dimension. This dehumanization of the worker led to abuses in the form of low wages and poor working conditions. Marxism arose as a response to these abuses, but because of its materialism, it failed to account adequately for the subjective dimension of work, contributing to the exploitation of workers under communist regimes decades later.[38]

Although clearly distinct, there is a similarity between critical realism's descriptive critique of Marxism's treatment of the individual agent within social structures and John Paul II's normative critique. In both cases, Marxism fails to treat the individual as "a conscious and free subject," capable of both self-direction and self-realization. Although some Catholics, including many Latin American liberation theologians, have claimed that Marxist social analysis can be separated from its more problematic philosophical elements, the link between these descriptive and normative critiques of Marxism lends credence to Pope Paul VI's warning in his 1971 apostolic letter *Octogesima adveniens* that there is an "intimate link" that binds together Marxist analysis and ideology.[39]

INSTITUTIONAL ECONOMICS AND CATHOLIC SOCIAL TEACHING

So far I have looked at how critical realism's treatment of the agency-structure problem closely mirrors Catholic social teaching's vision of the moral agency of the person in community. Critical realism and institutional economics offer descriptive critiques of both capitalism and Marxism that can enrich the teaching's long-standing normative criticism of those economic systems. Institutional economists have developed a way of thinking about the economy grounded in a critical realist methodology but addressing more complex questions of economic organization. In this section, I want to outline some of the fundamental points of this economic vision and how they can further improve Catholic social teaching.

Institutional economics suggests that we can ascribe three characteristics to the capitalist system: it is complex, nonlinear, and open.[40] First, any economy is made up of a complex mixture of individuals, organizations (business firms, banks, government agencies, labor unions, etc.), and institutions. The economy also has structural features, both at the domestic and global levels. Domestically, for example, the economy consists in different sectors (such as agriculture, manufacturing, and service), and globally the economy is structured by the relative wealth and level of development of different countries. Each of these elements of the global economy has causal power. Economic structures and institutions shape the decisions of individuals and economic organizations, but individuals and organizations maintain and transform those institutions and structures even as they interact with one another.[41] Because each of these elements has autonomous causal powers that interact with and shape one another, the economy is a *complex* system.

Why is this important? In the 1970s Latin American liberation theologians, drawing on the school of economic thought known as dependency theory, argued that Latin America's poverty was primarily caused by its peripheral position within the global economy. Forced into importing manufactured goods produced in the developed world while exporting raw materials and cheap goods in return, the developing world was left with stagnation and poverty. Oppressive authoritarian governments in Latin America reinforced the structures of the global economy and prevented the radical political changes that could subvert this system.[42] In contrast, others such as Michael Novak argued that global capitalism should not be blamed for the woes of Latin America precisely because the nations of Latin America were not capitalist. In this view, it was Latin America's archaic economic institutions, inherited from the Spanish and Portuguese colonial past, that kept Latin America from experiencing economic dynamism and growth.[43] If the global economy is a complex system, however, then there are elements of truth in both perspectives while they both fall short by thinking of the economic system as if it were by necessity simple and uniform. A nation's economic development is shaped by the interaction of global economic structures and the institutions of the domestic economy. To promote authentic development, a nation's people must work toward developing economic structures that promote economic initiative and creativity while also fostering a just distribution of goods and services; there must also be a global sense of solidarity in order to create an international economic order that better fosters the development of the world's poorer nations.

Second, the economy, at both global and national levels, is a nonlinear system, a characteristic closely linked to the economy's complexity. Because the course of the economy is shaped by the actions of countless individuals, organizations, governments, and the emergent properties of the system itself, it does not follow a set path.[44] Contrary to Marxism, the economic system does not evolve through preestablished, predictable stages. Moreover, contrary to mainstream economics, there is no "natural state" for the economy. Mainstream economics assumes that market institutions can be established by removing the obstacles, both governmental and cultural, that stand in the way of free market exchange. In reality, when new institutions are introduced into a country's economy, they interact with the already-existing economic institutions and cultural norms of that country in a variety of ways. Therefore, even despite the tendency of globalization to homogenize, there are "varieties of capitalism" dependent on the unique historical trajectories and ethical priorities of diverse nations.[45] Understanding a particular nation's economy and charting a path to development require understanding the nation's economic history and the evolution of its economic institutions.

Third, the economic system is open—in two distinct ways. On the one hand, the economic system is open because the human persons who engage in economic activity are irreducibly free beings, open to the transcendent. Although economic structures generate restrictions and opportunities that shape decisions, the economic system remains open to change over time because of the freedom of economic agents, and economic activity ultimately serves purposes that transcend the realm of economics. On the other hand, the economic system is open in that it depends on resources from outside of itself for its proper functioning.[46] The state and culture provide the legal institutions and social norms that shape economic behavior, and the state also structures economic activity and distributes economic resources. Economic production is dependent on the continued availability of natural resources and threatened by their depletion. Mainstream economics has often taken these resources for granted and ignored how the economy and natural environment influence one another.[47] Chapter 6 of this volume examines in more detail how this relationship impacts the crisis of climate change.

The notion of "integral ecology" found in Pope Francis's 2015 encyclical *Laudato si'* expresses a similar idea and can be enriched by institutional economics. First of all, Francis emphasizes the connection between humankind and the natural environment: "Nature cannot be regarded as something separate from ourselves or as a mere setting in which we live. We are part of nature, included in it and thus in constant interaction with it."[48] He then outlines a series of interconnected human ecologies: economic ecology, social ecology, cultural ecology, and the ecology of daily life.[49] By appealing to the metaphor of a natural ecosystem, Francis highlights the interconnectedness and mutual influence of social systems as well as the distinctiveness of each one. He also makes clear that our efforts to address social problems cannot focus on only one sphere of social life but must take an integral approach: "We are faced not with two separate crises, one environmental and the other social, but rather with one complex crisis which is both social and environmental."[50] In *Laudato si',* Pope Francis provides a compelling vision of social life and humanity's connection to the natural environment. Critical realism and institutional economics offer analytical tools to help us study and transform social life guided by that vision.

CONCLUSION

Throughout its long history, Catholic social teaching has drawn on a variety of economic and sociological schools of thought to enrich its teachings on economic life and to enable Catholics to translate their faith commitments into practical economic policies. In the twenty-first century, critical realism can serve as a helpful dialogue partner that can deepen the Catholic Church's understanding of its own teachings on the economy and point toward new directions for the development of that teaching. Likewise, institutional economics, particularly when built on the foundations of critical realism, offers a way of thinking about the economy that both complements and challenges Catholic thinking on economic life. It is the aim of this volume to demonstrate to the reader just how much promise such conversations offer to Christian ethical reflection.

NOTES

1. See, for example, Normand J. Paulhus, "Social Catholicism and the Fribourg Union," *Annual of the Society of Christian Ethics*, 1980, 63–88, http://hdl.handle.net/10822 /786185.
2. Kees van Kersbergen, *Social Capitalism: A Study of Christian Democracy and the Welfare State* (New York: Routledge, 1995).
3. Second Vatican Council, *Gaudium et spes* (1965), 12, 19, http://www.vatican.va/archive /hist_councils/ii_vatican_council/documents/vat-ii_const_19651207_gaudium-et-spes _en.html.
4. Second Vatican Council, *Gaudium et spes*, 25.
5. Second Vatican Council, 26.
6. Second Vatican Council, 25.
7. John Paul II, *Centesimus annus* (1991), 35, http://w2.vatican.va/content/john-paul-ii/en /encyclicals/documents/hf_jp-ii_enc_01051991_centesimus-annus.html.
8. Margaret S. Archer, *Realist Social Theory: The Morphogenetic Approach* (New York: Cambridge University Press, 1995), 165–84.
9. Archer, 34–46; and Geoffrey M. Hodgson, *The Evolution of Institutional Economics: Agency, Structure, and Darwinism in American Institutionalism* (New York: Routledge, 2004), 16–23.
10. Archer, *Realist Social Theory*, 46–57; and Hodgson, *Evolution of Institutional Economics*, 23–28.
11. Archer, *Realist Social Theory*, 93–134.
12. Geoffrey M. Hodgson, *Conceptualizing Capitalism: Institutions, Evolution, Future* (Chicago: University of Chicago Press, 2015), 57–59.
13. Milton Friedman, "The Methodology of Positive Economics," in *Essays in Positive Economics* (Chicago: University of Chicago Press, 1966), 3–43.
14. Quoted in Hodgson, *Evolution of Institutional Economics*, 20.
15. Hodgson, 16–23.
16. Karl Polanyi, *The Great Transformation* (New York: Farrar & Rinehart, 1944).

17. Hodgson, *Conceptualizing Capitalism*, 101–11.
18. Thomas Aquinas, *Summa Theologica*, I-II, q. 94, a.5.
19. See, for example, Paul VI's *Populorum progressio* (1967), 18–19, http://w2.vatican.va /content/paul-vi/en/encyclicals/documents/hf_p-vi_enc_26031967_populorum.html.
20. John Paul II, *Sollicitudo rei socialis* (1987), 28, http://w2.vatican.va/content/john-paul-ii /en/encyclicals/documents/hf_jp-ii_enc_30121987_sollicitudo-rei-socialis.html.
21. John Paul II, *Centesimus annus*, 36.
22. Richard John Neuhaus, *Doing Well & Doing Good: The Challenge to the Christian Capitalist* (New York: Doubleday, 1992), 224–25.
23. John Paul II, *Centesimus annus*, 38–39.
24. John Paul II, 39.
25. John Paul II, 51.
26. Archer, *Realist Social Theory*, 305.
27. Indeed, an earlier institutional economist, John Kenneth Galbraith, produced one of the seminal works on consumerism, *The Affluent Society* (Boston: Houghton-Mifflin, 1958).
28. Karl Marx, "The 18th Brumaire of Louis Bonaparte," in *Surveys from Exile: Political Writings*, vol. 2, ed. David Fernbach (Harmondsworth, UK: Penguin, 1973), 146.
29. Karl Marx, *Capital*, vol. 3, trans. David Fernbach (Harmondsworth, UK: Pelican, 1981), 1019–20.
30. Hodgson, *Evolution of Institutional Economics*, 24–25.
31. Hodgson, 27–28.
32. Karl Marx, *A Contribution to the Critique of Political Economy*, trans. S. W. Ryazanskaya, ed. Maurice Dobb (London: Lawrence and Wishart, 1971), 20–21.
33. Hodgson finds Thorstein Veblen's account of this process superior to Marx's. See Hodgson, *Evolution of Institutional Economics*, 181–84.
34. John Paul II, *Centesimus annus*, 12.
35. John Paul II, *Laborem exercens* (1981), 4–5, http://w2.vatican.va/content/john-paul-ii/en /encyclicals/documents/hf_jp-ii_enc_14091981_laborem-exercens.html.
36. John Paul II, 6.
37. John Paul II, 12.
38. John Paul II, 11.
39. Paul VI, *Octogesima adveniens* (1971), 34, http://w2.vatican.va/content/paul-vi/en/apost _letters/documents/hf_p-vi_apl_19710514_octogesima-adveniens.html.
40. I explore these characteristics in more detail in Matthew Shadle, *Interrupting Capitalism: Catholic Social Thought and the Economy* (New York: Oxford University Press, 2018), 27–29.
41. Hodgson, *Conceptualizing Capitalism*, 317–18.
42. See, for example, Gustavo Gutiérrez, *A Theology of Liberation: History, Politics, and Salvation*, rev. ed., trans. Sr. Caridad Inda and John Eagleson (Maryknoll, NY: Orbis, 1988), 49–54.
43. For example, see Michael Novak, *The Spirit of Democratic Capitalism*, 2nd ed. (Lanham, MD: Madison Books, 1991), 276–82.
44. Geoffrey Hodgson, *Economics in the Shadows of Darwin and Marx: Essays on Institutional and Evolutionary Themes* (Northampton, MA: Edward Elgar, 2006), 68.
45. Hodgson, *Conceptualizing Capitalism*, 32, 325–27.

46. Archer, *Realist Social Theory*, 69–70.
47. Tony Lawson, *Economics and Reality* (New York: Routledge, 1997), 63.
48. Francis, *Laudato si'* (2015), 139, http://w2.vatican.va/content/francesco/en/encyclicals/documents/papa-francesco_20150524_enciclica-laudato-si.html.
49. Francis, 137–55.
50. Francis, 139.

CHAPTER 8

Critical Realism, Virtue Ethics, and Moral Agency

Daniel J. Daly

A 2008 study found that the "floor" for carbon consumption for an American was 8.5 metric tons per year. This was the estimated carbon footprint of a person suffering from homelessness, who eats in soup kitchens and sleeps in shelters. Tellingly, this figure also includes each US citizen's share of carbon usage due to the array of government services available to everyone, including police, roads, libraries, the court system, and the military. The global average at the time was 4 tons per year; the US average was estimated at 20 tons.[1] The authors of the study concluded that reaching the global average "is not obtainable for the average American on a voluntary basis."[2]

Most Christian ethicists take it for granted that a high carbon footprint is less ecologically virtuous than a low carbon footprint. But, as the study claimed, Americans are incapable of even reaching the global average due to the structural constraints that are out of their control. What is a virtue ethicist to make of this finding? In chapter 6 David Cloutier argues that Christian ethicists will be able to produce sharper analyses of the ethics of climate change through an engagement with critical realism. Reflecting Cloutier's insight, the purpose of this chapter is to suggest some of the ways in which critical realism aids in a virtue analysis of problems such as climate change.

Problems like these force virtue ethicists to contend with the structural forces that constrain virtuous activities and encourage vicious ones, forces that profoundly shape moral agency. However, as I show in the first part of this chapter, virtue ethicists have inadequately attended to the sociological realities that would help them navigate such problems. The second part offers critical realism as a tool for virtue ethicists. More specifically, critical realism provides virtue ethicists a clearer understanding of how social structures shape moral agency regarding both action and character. Third, I briefly outline six ways critical realist sociology can contribute to research within virtue ethics. Finally, the chapter offers a "call for papers," noting nine areas needing further research in the relationship of critical realism and virtue ethics.

Two further introductory comments are in order. First, it is helpful to distinguish between virtue ethics and virtue theory. Virtue ethics is a normative theory in which the virtues constitute the lenses through which human action and character are morally evaluated. Virtue ethicists ask, "Does one become ecologically unjust if one drives an SUV?" and "How might a just and loving person respond to hate speech?" A virtue theory, on the other hand, is the meta-ethics of virtue ethics; it explains what a virtue is and how virtue is formed. A strong and insightful virtue ethics relies on a well-developed virtue theory.[3] This chapter is more of an exercise in the latter than the former, although what it has to say also will be quite helpful normatively.

Second, readers will find that the chapter focuses almost exclusively on social structures, not on culture. This occurs because of the constraints of space in a primer and because structure presents the more promising opportunity for both virtue theory and virtue ethics. Nonetheless, the critical realist analysis of culture provided by Matthew Shadle in chapter 5 also promises to deepen our understanding of the relation of virtue and culture.

A PROBLEM WITH VIRTUE ETHICS

Virtue theorist Julia Annas has written that virtue can be understood only in relation to how it is acquired.[4] We come to know what a character trait is, partially, through a description of how the trait was cultivated and sustained by the person. This insight invites virtue ethicists to inquire about the state of the field regarding the formation of the virtues. In their 2015 article titled "The Resurgence of Virtue in Recent Moral Theology," David Cloutier and William Mattison argue that the formation of a person's character within a community is the "least developed theme in virtue ethics."[5] This is a problem for Christian virtue ethics, given its theoanthropological commitment to the social nature of the person. Christian virtue ethicists know *that* the moral agency of persons is formed within community; they just have yet to analyze *how* this transpires.

The issue of how communities shape the moral character of their members requires virtue ethicists to investigate the social realities of community life. However, virtue ethics has had an uneven relationship to the social sciences. Virtue ethicists have regularly turned to psychology to make sense of how character takes root in a person.[6] By comparison, virtue ethics has been sociologically undertheorized. The turn to the person and relationality that was representative of Christian ethics in the second half of the twentieth century has not been accompanied by a parallel turn to the social, to what sociologists call the "structure-agency" problem. The problem is this: What is the relationship of social structure and human agency? There are a number of potential sociological solutions to this problem, but Christian ethicists have typically opted for none of them.

Take, for instance, the two seminal texts in the retrieval of virtue ethics, Alasdair MacIntyre's *After Virtue* and Stanley Hauerwas's *A Community of Character*. Christopher Vogt argues that the majority of Christian virtue ethicists have adopted MacIntyre's tripartite approach to the formation of virtue.[7] Virtues, according to MacIntyre's account, are formed through the practices, narratives, and overarching moral tradition of a community.[8] Less recognized by virtue ethicists are MacIntyre's claims that social institutions can foster or endanger the virtues, and that the pursuit of the virtues for an individual person will be in relation to the social roles—such as son, professor, American citizen—that one inhabits.[9] The focus on the former set of insights as opposed to the latter is understandable because MacIntyre provides a penetrating analysis of the ethical concepts that he introduced (practice, narrative, tradition), while he gives only a cursory treatment of the sociostructural realities of institution and role. MacIntyre uses these sociological concepts in a colloquial, informal manner. While he is sure that social roles shape moral character, he does not say how they do so.

Hauerwas argues that Christians have failed to produce the conceptual categories needed to make sense of moral development. His solution is to turn to narrative and virtue, explaining that people need a story-formed community to acquire the virtues. "What we need is not a principle or end but a narrative that charts a way for us to live coherently amid the diversity and conflicts that circumscribe and shape our moral existence."[10] That story must be a true story, which for Christians is found in the Scripture. As with MacIntyre, we find substantial contributions to virtue ethics in Hauerwas's work. But, like MacIntyre, his virtue theory needs to be more fully sociologized. Hauerwas acknowledges the psychology of moral development in his treatment of Kohlberg and briefly mentions that the "professions" (such as medicine and law) provide something analogous to a school of virtue. But more needs to be said. Most pressingly, what is community, and how do the members of a community use narrative to shape the character of its members? Hauerwas, like MacIntyre, would benefit from a sociological account of social life.

Such imprecision and lack of depth regarding concepts such as role, structure, institution, and community is commonplace in Christian ethics. *Gaudium et spes* is representative of magisterial teaching in this way. The Council Fathers claimed that "when the structure of affairs is flawed by the consequences of sin, man, already born with a bent toward evil, finds there new inducements to sin, which cannot be overcome without strenuous efforts and the assistance of grace."[11] How flawed structures induce people to sin is not explained, and, as Theodora Hawksley observes in chapter 2, simply rearranging the traditional elements of Catholic social teaching will not do the job.

Further, the one attempt at a definition of structure in Catholic social teaching was unsuccessful. The Congregation for the Doctrine of the Faith's 1986 "Instruction on Christian Liberation" wrote that structures

are the sets of institutions and practices which people find already existing or which they create, on the national and international level, and which orientate or organize economic, social and political life. Being necessary in themselves, they often tend to become fixed and fossilized as mechanisms relatively independent of the human will, thereby paralyzing or distorting social development and causing injustice. However, they always depend on the responsibility of man, who can alter them, and not upon an alleged determinism of history.[12]

No social theorist has defined "structure" in such terms. Notice that structures are first "fossilized," and "relatively independent of the human will," and then "paralyze social development" and can be "alter(ed)" by the human will. Clearly, more needs to be said about the relationship of social structures and personal moral agency.

Contemporary Christian theologians have only occasionally delved into social theory. In a book that was notable for its sociological depth, Mark O'Keefe drew on Peter Berger and Thomas Luckmann's *The Social Construction of Reality* to argue that "social sin . . . may also dispose individuals to further personal sin."[13] My own work has previously employed Berger and Luckmann to make similar claims.[14] However, the dialectical approach developed by Berger and Luckmann contains several problems that I now believe are corrected in critical realism.[15]

This lack of insight regarding social realities has led Daniel Finn to claim that "Catholic social thought has no coherent account of what a social structure is."[16] The same is true throughout Christian ethics, including virtue ethics. For reasons such as these, Christopher Vogt argues that virtue ethicists needed to more fully draw on the social sciences.[17]

Compare this state of affairs to most Christian approaches to medical ethics, where ethicists lean on the best medical science as a precondition for making normative claims. Medical ethicists rightly realize that they must first understand the reality of the embryo or the progression of end-stage liver failure before they develop the ethics of abortion or liver transplantation. In contrast, virtue ethicists claim that personal character is formed in and through community and social structures but rarely, if ever, turn to social science to explain how community and structure shape the moral agency of persons.

STRUCTURE, AGENCY, AND VIRTUE ETHICS

Given that chapters 3 and 4 describe emergence, stratifications, and social structures, here I present two additional elements of critical realist thought that are particularly useful for virtue ethics: the position-practice system and normative social institutions.

Position-Practice System

Recall that according to critical realists, structures are "systems of human relations among social positions."[18] In chapter 4, Daniel Finn notes that "the invisible relation between two social positions exerts causal impact on the persons who enter into them." As a result, social relations influence the deliberations, activities, and practices—the moral agency—of the members of the relation. In an early articulation of critical realist thought, Roy Bhaskar describes the mechanics of how this happens. Bhaskar argues that social positions are practice-laden.

> We need a system of mediating concepts . . . designating the slots, as it were, in the social structure into which active subjects must slip in order to reproduce it; that is, a system of concepts designating the point of contact between human agency and social structures. Such a point, liking acting to structure, must both endure and be immediately occupied by individuals. It is clear that the mediating system we need is that of the positions (places, functions, rules, tasks, duties, rights, etc.) occupied (filled, assumed, enacted, etc.) by individuals and of the practices (activities, etc.) in which, in virtue of their occupancy of these positions they engage. I shall call this mediating system the position-practice system. Now such positions and practices, if they are to be individuated at all, can only be done so relationally.[19]

The position-practice system is crucial in understanding how structures shape the activity of position holders. Here Bhaskar argues that when a person assumes a social position (e.g., professor) she typically enters into a relation with another position holder (e.g., dean) who will hold her accountable to the practices that constitute the position. The position of professor contains practices that a dean will expect such a professor to perform: teaching, grading, meeting with students, researching, writing, and publishing papers.

While the relation of dean to professor enables and constrains the agency of the latter, it also constrains and enables the agency of the dean. Only a shortsighted dean would consistently ignore or disparage faculty. The faculty may not have the capacity formally to punish the dean if she fails to perform her position well, but they can and do apply social pressure to the dean to do so. The relation of dean-faculty enables and constrains the activities of both parties.

Virtue ethicists will be interested to note that social relations enable and constrain moral agency. Margaret Archer has emphasized that while persons retain free will, their relations to other position holders generate enablements and constraints on their actions.[20] Social relations enable, facilitate, and reward specific activities while they constrain, discourage, and penalize others, punishing those who "malpractice" the position. Professors are enabled to perform the above practices and are constrained from failing to do so. That is, a professor would be disciplined by the dean if, for instance, he stopped giving grades to students and would be penalized by student disapproval if he droned on in boring, uninformed lectures. Similarly, the professor would be worse off if he neglected to take up advantages offered to those in his position, such as funding to attend professional conferences to present papers. Critical realists emphasize that position holders retain free will; professors are not hydraulically moved to give grades or to develop interesting class modules.[21] They can choose not to. However, if they fail to perform these practices, there are negative consequences, ranging from student dissatisfaction to the loss of their jobs. Most people, most of the time, "go along" with the practices required of them, thereby sustaining the social structures they inhabit.

The essential point is that the relations among social positions enable and constrain the decisions of those who inhabit a social position. These enablements and constraints are durable and regularized; they invite position holders to consistently and habitually perform certain activities, and they discourage other activities. In short, participation in a structure presents a prime opportunity to acquire habits. Some habits will be technical. Professors learn how to deliver more effective lectures and strengthen their research skills. Other habits will be moral, as when certain structures constrain or enable one's ability to relate well to God, neighbor, self, and creation. As the example at the outset showed, participation in American structures of consumption constrains an American's ability to be ecologically just.

Normative Social Institutions, Norm Circles, and Organizations

Dave Elder-Vass uses a critical realist lens to take a more granular look at social reality. Elder-Vass analyzes two principal kinds of structures that people encounter on a daily basis: normative social institutions and organizations.[22]

Normative social institutions are one type of social structure that "refers to arrangements involving large numbers of people whose behavior is guided by norms and roles."[23] Elder-Vass emphasizes that social institutions are normative because they emerge from what he calls "norm circles." The people who participate in the normative social institution do so by entering the norm circle. Here the institution is quite loose and is not reducible to the nation-state or any municipality. Instead, it is a real but unorganized institution that exists among members of a community.

Norm circles are made of people who share, endorse, and enforce a set of beliefs and dispositions.[24] Norm circles can be proximal (the people around you), imagined (such as a nation or ethnicity), or actual (the actual people who endorse the beliefs and dispositions of the circle). Take, for example, driving in the United States. While there are laws that define legal driving practices, there is also a normative social institution that exists among drivers in places like Boston. This institution has emerged through the organic creation of a "Boston drivers' norm circle." In Boston, one is expected to drive somewhat aggressively, accelerating as soon as the light turns green and quickly merging onto the highway. The key norm in this circle is that one is not to slow down others and the flow of traffic. Such driving habits are not legislated, but they do exist among the members of the Boston drivers' norm circle. Drivers who fail to exercise these habits will be sanctioned by the members of the norm circle through honking, yelling, and other gestures. As Elder-Vass notes, "As a consequence of being members of a norm circle, then, these individuals act differently than they would do otherwise."[25] Eventually, people who drive in Boston, whether or not they first learned to drive there, are likely to conform to the norm circle and acquire new moral habits of relation to other drivers.

Another type of structure is the organization.[26] Whereas normative social institutions are fairly loose and membership is fluid, organizations are a kind of association. Organizations differ from mere associations insofar as they are highly complex and contain authority roles and relations. While there is no president of an association, there is of a college or multinational corporation. Like any association, organizations have causal power. When a person assumes position in an organization they also assume the activities that have been specified in the role by the organization. Each organizational role has some flexibility, but only to a point. Again, a person's moral agency is both enabled and constrained when she belongs to an organization.

Normative social institutions and organizations shape the activities and moral character of their members. They provide smooth pathways to certain kinds of activities and produce barriers to others. Again, the prescribed and proscribed activities are durable and, thus, over time encourage the acquisition of certain character traits and discourage others. While it is not impossible for a Boston driver to cultivate patience and generosity toward other commuters, it surely is more difficult than for drivers living in a small Midwest community with a norm circle grounded in courtesy and cooperation.

SOME USES OF CRITICAL REALISM IN VIRTUE ETHICS

Recall the problems endemic to virtue ethics presented in the first part of this chapter. There I note that character formation is the least-developed theme in virtue ethics, which has given short shrift to social theory. Critical realism addresses these problems in six significant ways.

First, critical realism enables virtue ethicists to more fully understand moral agency. As I note above, just as good medical ethics relies on an understanding of medical realities, so too good virtue ethics is grounded on an accurate account of social realities. As this volume shows, critical realism offers a precise account of what a social structure is and how it shapes personal agency. In other words, it offers a rigorous solution to the structure-agency problem. Critical realism maintains that social structures and personal moral agency are distinct but that social structures are causes (among others) of human action. Structures do not "infect" the person and his habits as some social theories claim, but they do exist as causal influences on moral decisions. The engagement with critical realism reveals that any explanation of moral agency that ignores social structures is deficient.

Second, the precision of the critical realist solution to the structure-agency problem helps virtue ethicists better understand how a person's character is formed in community, addressing the central problem of contemporary virtue ethics. There are other influences in character formation, to be sure, but sociostructural formation must be included in any adequate description. Social structures influence daily decisions for good or ill, and over time this influence is habit forming; it shapes who we are. Structures influence practices that, when enacted, become the practitioner. Agents become either virtuous or vicious in and through the structures they inhabit.

Third, the realization that social structures play a causal role in a person's actions and in subsequent shaping of moral character reveals the fully emergent nature of trait development. Character emerges from within the relation of a person's actions, intentions, motivations, emotions, reasoning, and willing as well as social structures and cultural factors such as how one was parented and one's religion and schooling. Importantly, character cannot be reduced to any one of these. The concept of emergence, described by Daniel Finn in chapter 3, helps virtue ethicists more fully understand and articulate what moral character is and the complexities of its formation. This helps virtue ethicists address the issue that Julia Annas has articulated— namely, that the nature of the virtues is found in how virtues are formed. The notion that the virtues, as character traits, are emergent realities is, in my estimation, a conceptual move forward. Such a move is made possible by the development of the emergentist notion of reality that was developed through critical realism, outlined in chapters 3 and 4.

An emergentist theory of character development and acquisition moves the field away from the reductionistic accounts found in intellectualist and voluntarist virtue theories as well as in those that see virtue as the simple aggregation of a person's actions. Because a person's moral decision-making matters, so do the structures that constrain and enable that decision-making. Notice that I am not arguing that social structures excuse decision-making contrary to virtue. I am only arguing that, in fact, social structures play a causal role in the moral decisions that people make. Because structures enable and constrain action, they must be considered when describing how it is that a person's character is formed in community.

Fourth, critical realism helps virtue ethicists see that social structures enable and constrain certain moral traits as well as how they do this. This opens up a less abstract understanding of the virtues, a more contextual one. Even well-meaning Americans are less ecologically just than they otherwise would have been because of the web of relations in which they are implicated. An American's eco-injustice is in part structurally caused.

The fifth point moves in a different direction. Thus far I have highlighted how critical realism helps virtue ethics more fully explain how structures shape moral character. In addition to these, critical realism helps virtue ethicists understand that and how virtuous persons act virtuously from within what Elder-Vass has called "cross-cutting" structures. A cross-cutting structure contains values, relations, and norms that conflict with those of an individual person. For example, pro-life Catholic Democrats exist in a cross-cutting situation where the relation to the unborn prescribed by Church and party conflict dramatically.

In this way, critical realism illuminates the moral ambiguity of daily life. Virtuous people have, at times, limited opportunities to act virtuously. As Julia Annas wrote, people often exhibit only as much virtue as their society allows.[27] Due to structural enablements and constraints, virtuous people will often have to pay a serious price if they choose to avoid harming their relations with others and the natural world. This, I believe, should steer ethicists away from ideal notions of virtue toward a notion that comports with the difficulties of living the virtues within cross-cutting structures. The question that one should ask is, What would a person of virtuous character do given these structural constraints? We may still want to maintain that a perfectly virtuous person would refuse to participate in structures that diminished her active love of God, others, and the natural world. However, virtuously perfect institutions are at least as rare as perfectly virtuous persons. Heroic refusal is not required for the virtuous life.

Alasdair MacIntyre argues that "we discover our character in tension with what our society and our roles ask of us."[28] Again, such a claim needs refinement. A critical realist lens shows that character is forged in response to the structural constraints and enablements that confront us. For example, while a person of the highest ecological moral character may choose to live off the grid, ecologically virtuous persons can still opt to live "on the grid" but in a way in which they habitually attempt to minimize their carbon use, waste production, and overall eco-harm. This is the case because of the multiplicity of relations and goods with which the virtuous person should concern himself. Such a person will not only account for the health of the environment but also the well-being of his children and his relationships with others and God.

Critical realism helps to unveil the complex nature of the virtuous life. Navigating such complexity requires a compass—an overall direction to one's moral life in the form of an ordered notion of goods. It also requires skills of navigation—prudence, which enables the person to discover the best way to those goods.

Sixth, integrating social theory helps to theorize virtue ethics. Earlier I argued that virtue has been sociologically undertheorized. If one removes the qualifier "sociologically," one still has a true statement. While virtue ethics depends on a robust and coherent virtue theory, as I argued earlier, contemporary theological articulations of virtue ethics are typically theoretically thin. A turn to critical realism invites virtue ethicists to engage in metaethical questions and not just use the virtues to make normative claims about character and action. In short, the engagement with critical realism provides a more developed virtue theory.

Virtue has tended to focus on how culture shapes character; narrative, tradition, and practice all play a role. But so, too, do the hard surfaces of structural enablements and constraints. Critical realism shows that MacIntyre's cultural explanation of character formation is necessary but incomplete. Structure and culture—the two major dimensions of social life—each require attention from virtue ethicists.

A CALL FOR PAPERS

If Christian virtue ethics is to continue to mature increasingly, it will need to attend to questions of virtue theory and specifically to the ways in which moral character is shaped by social structures. In the spirit of initiating a conversation among virtue ethicists regarding critical realism, I conclude the chapter by suggesting avenues for further exploration.

First, critical realism invites questions regarding either the absolute or relative nature of the virtues. For instance, is ecological virtue a trait that shows itself in comparison to the prevailing lifestyle, such that it is possible to be only relatively (i.e., more or less) ecologically just, as opposed to absolutely ecologically just? Should we expect the Dutch to be more ecologically virtuous than Americans and thus hold them to a higher standard of virtue?

Second, how does critical realism help virtue ethicists understand the action and moral character of persons who experience radically constrained agency? Here I am thinking of the Dalit of India or of destitute women throughout the world who use prostitution to support themselves and their children. Do the relations and positions in which they exist form their moral character? For example, how might Lisa Tessman's important notion of "burdened virtues" be helped by a critical realist description of the structural realities that so profoundly constrain the moral agency of vulnerable peoples throughout the world?

Third, does the critical realist explanation of social structures and constrained/enabled agency comport with liberationist understandings of social structures and how they shape moral character?

Fourth, do social structures themselves possess a certain moral character, or are they all morally neutral? Might it be possible to categorize relations or positions as virtuous or vicious?

Fifth, given the critical realist view of social reality, will virtue ethicists find value in manualist-era principles such as cooperation or tolerance in addressing how agents should act in the presence of structural evils? Do such principles retain value, or are new principles needed given our new knowledge of social structures?

Sixth, how might those who scrutinize globalization through a virtue lens benefit from the critical realist notion of relationality as "reciprocal action among two entities?" Can critical realism illuminate what living a life of global solidarity and justice looks like?

Seventh, what are the actions and habits that contemporary normative social institutions and organizations are cultivating in their members?

Eighth, how might professional virtue ethics benefit from the critical realist conceptual framework? For example, do the more precise notions of structure, organizations, and the position-practice system supplement the rather nebulous idea of "corporate culture" that is currently in use in professional ethics?

Finally, what are the implications for moral formation that are present in critical realism? How should one form the character of oneself and one's children in light of these findings? If social structures constrain and enable action, and therefore character, what does this say about how to shape the character of children? Should parents and mentors prevent the young from inhabiting positions that make the cultivation of virtue more difficult? Must we move toward a "virtue in rags" approach in which the virtuous life is presented as one of extreme sacrifice for the sake of pursuing the good, or is there virtue to be found in moral compromise, as some authors have recently suggested?[29]

These are but a few of the questions that critical realism raises for virtue ethicists. The continued explanatory capacity and output power of virtue ethics will depend, in part, on how the guild addresses them.

NOTES

1. "Carbon Footprint of Best Conserving Americans Is Still Double Global Average," *ScienceDaily*, accessed September 20, 2017, https://www.sciencedaily.com/releases /2008/04/080428120658.htm.

2. Timothy Gutowski, Amanda Taplett, Anna Allen, Amy Banzaert, Rob Cirinciore, Christopher Cleaver, Stacy Figueredo, et al., "Environmental Life Style Analysis (ELSA)," presentation, IEEE International Symposium on Electronics and the Environment, San Francisco, May 19–20, 2008, http://web.mit.edu/ebm/www/Publications/ELSA %20IEEE%202008.pdf.

3. Nancy Snow, "Models of Virtue," in *The Routledge Companion to Virtue Ethics*, ed. Lorraine Besser and Michael Slote (New York: Routledge, 2015), 259.

4. Julia Annas, *Intelligent Virtue* (Oxford: Oxford University Press, 2011), 28.

5. Annas, 231.

6. See Julia Annas, Darcia Narvaez, and Nancy E. Snow, eds. *Developing the Virtues: Integrating Perspectives* (New York: Oxford University Press, 2016); and Nancy E. Snow, ed. *Cultivating Virtue: Perspectives from Philosophy, Theology, and Psychology* (New York: Oxford, 2014).

7. Christopher Vogt, "Virtue: Personal Formation and Social Transformation," *Theological Studies* 77 (2016): 188.

8. Alasdair MacIntyre, *After Virtue* (Notre Dame, IN: University of Notre Dame Press, 1981), chap. 14.

9. MacIntyre, 195, 220.

10. Stanley Hauerwas, *A Community of Character: Toward a Constructive Christian Social Ethic* (Notre Dame, IN: University of Notre Dame Press, 1981), 114.

11. Second Vatican Council, *Gaudium et spes* (December 7, 1965), § 25, http://www.vatican .va/archive/hist_councils/ii_vatican_council/documents/vat-ii_cons_19651207_gaudium -et-spes_en.html.

12. Congregation for the Doctrine of the Faith, "Instruction on Christian Freedom and Liberation," § 74, accessed August 2, 2017, http://www.vatican.va/roman_curia/congregations /cfaith/documents/rc_con_cfaith_doc_19860322_freedom-liberation_en.html.

13. Mark O'Keefe, *What Are They Saying about Social Sin?* (New York: Paulist Press, 1990), 62.

14. Daniel J. Daly, "Structures of Virtue and Vice," *New Blackfriars* 92 (2011).

15. See Roy Bhaskar, *The Possibility of Naturalism: A Philosophical Critique of the Contemporary Human Sciences* (Atlantic Highlands, NJ: Humanities Press, 1979), 40–47; and Christian Smith, *What Is a Person? Rethinking Humanity, Social Life, and the Moral Good from the Person Up* (Chicago: University of Chicago Press, 2010), 174.

16. Daniel Finn, "What Is a Sinful Social Structure?," *Theological Studies* 77 (2016): 138.

17. Vogt, "Virtue," 195. In the interest of full disclosure, Vogt's call for a greater engagement with the social sciences occurs in a section in which he is critiquing an article of mine. He notes that the social theory that I used in "Structures of Virtue and Vice," is outdated. The present essay is an attempt to correct that shortcoming.
18. Douglas V. Porpora, "Four Concepts of Social Structure," *Journal for the Theory of Social Behavior* 19, no. 2 (1989): 195.
19. Bhaskar, *Possibility of Naturalism*, 51.
20. Margaret Archer, introduction to *Structure, Agency, and the Internal Conversation* (New York: Cambridge University Press, 2003).
21. Archer, 1.
22. Dave Elder-Vass, *The Causal Power of Social Structures* (New York: Cambridge University Press, 2011), 195.
23. Elder-Vass, 117.
24. Elder-Vass, chap. 6.
25. Elder-Vass, 124.
26. Elder-Vass, chap. 7.
27. Annas, *Intelligent Virtue*, 46.
28. Alasdair MacIntyre, "Social Structures and Their Threats to Moral Agency," *Philosophy* 74 (1999): 321.
29. D. M. Yeager and Stewart Herman, "The Virtue of 'Selling Out': Compromise as a Moral Transaction," *Journal of the Society of Christian Ethics* 37 (2017).

AFTERWORD

Lisa Sowle Cahill

The problem of moral agency has had a long and rocky road in Christian ethics, beginning with Paul's famous lament, "For the good that I would, I do not: but the evil which I would not, that I do" (Rom. 7:19). That road took a decisive turn with Augustine's retort to Pelagius that whereas some might think that "righteous living is a matter of our own making . . . this also is a divine work" (arguably an overcorrection).[1] Whether humans have moral freedom, or to what extent they do, is a high-stakes question for ethics. Control over "righteous living" is a basic ethical premise, as captured in Immanuel Kant's view that "ought implies can." Aquinas seems to strike a balance between moral freedom and external conditioning by linking moral responsibility to right practical reason and the virtue of prudence, and by interpreting grace as transforming, not replacing, moral capacities.[2] Yet in recent times, Augustine's pessimism about moral free will has been given new life by sociobiology and neuroscience, showing the effect of genes and brain activity on moral behavior (including the *libido dominandi*) and highlighting the overriding role of the emotions in setting the course of moral reason and eliciting moral judgments.[3]

Still another set of long-standing challenges comes from the direction of social, cultural, or economic determinism, in stronger and milder forms from Karl Marx through Ernst Troeltsch, H. Richard Niebuhr, and Peter Berger and Thomas Luckmann.[4] Few today would dispute that worldviews and ideas are highly indebted to the social contexts of their adherents. In fact, their interdependence is embraced by liberation and contextual theologies in the inevitable and important reciprocity of all theory and praxis. The challenge for theological ethics is to articulate precisely how and to what degree theories, more comprehensive systems of meaning, and the identities of persons and communities are generated by historical conditions and practices and still to show convincingly that persons and communities have adequate freedom to exercise agency in their own right. This volume, introducing "critical realist" sociology to the world of theological ethics, marks a huge advance in that regard. Moreover, critical realism grounds and explains the operation of social structures so essential to the goals of social transformation that define contemporary political theology and social ethics.

The two introductory chapters, by David Cloutier and Theodora Hawksley, argue persuasively that contemporary social ethics, Catholic and Protestant, would be strengthened by employing this perspective. Hawksley, for example, makes clear that Catholic social teaching has mistakenly described social evil in an "additive" way; structures of sin are understood as "the fruit of many sins." She helpfully illustrates the inadequacy of this additive view of social evil by quoting Joseph Liechty and Cecelia Clegg on sectarianism in Northern Ireland: "A sectarian system can be maintained by people who, individually, do not have a sectarian bone in their bodies."[5]

Cloutier explains that critical realism provides a way to understand how cultures and the social structures embedded within them shape the characters of persons and their actions; yet at the same time, these exist only because of those persons. A social structure is a system of relations among social positions along with the material conditions necessary to their coordination and efficacy over space and time. The agency of persons and the causal force of structures are neither mutually exclusive nor reducible to one another. Instead, they are mutually constituting: individuals exercise conditional power, while structures set the conditions by presenting people within them with restrictions and opportunities. But the causal influence of structures goes back to the agency of individuals because social structures arose, whether or not by design, from the actions of persons in the first place.

The crucial concept of "emergence" (Daniel Finn, chapters 3 and especially 4) helps explain how social structures can be said to have arisen from the action of persons and groups but exist "at a higher level." Just as water emerges from hydrogen and oxygen and has properties neither of those elements possesses, so structures differ qualitatively from the persons and groups that interacted to form them and have causal impact different from theirs. Structures, institutions, and organizations are necessary to the creation of broadly effective social agency of persons but can be either virtuous or vicious, depending on what sorts of actions their restrictions discourage and their opportunities encourage. People remain free to violate restrictions (although they will pay a price), to ignore some opportunities (forgoing a benefit), and to negotiate new opportunities, depending on their own priorities. As Gandhi and Martin Luther King Jr. showed, if enough people are willing to pay the price, social structures can be transformed from below.

Daniel Daly cites Douglas Porpora to the effect that "structures are 'systems of human relations among social positions,'" implying both that individuals are shaped by their place within the system, including their role-required actions, and that they have, within limits, the power to ratify, resist, or reform the relations and systems of relations in which they participate.[6] This is because their positions are "practice-laden," offering points of contact and influence between individuals and structures. One characteristic of a structure is the tendency to provide continuity to agency, and structures are predisposed to sustain continuity. Structures both constrain individual agency and establish possibilities for agency within existing channels. Established rules, channels of purpose and action, and the commitment or vested interest of others in maintaining them make structures inherently averse to reform. It is hard to get momentum for change in structures. This can be a good thing in a virtuous structure, but it is also why unjust structures are very successful at incentivizing and perpetuating vicious behavior. The power of individuals to subvert or reform structures is enhanced when it derives from or attracts the cooperation of fellow structure-resisters, acting either internally or externally to the structure or institution in question.

Authors Daniel Finn, David Cloutier, Matthew Shadle, and Daniel Daly skillfully and persuasively show how the framework of critical realism applies across a number of areas key to Christian social ethics, especially culture, the economy, and the environment, while also touching on racial and gender equality (Shadle). In all these areas, moral agents are shaped and constrained by social structures but retain transformative power from within. In addition, virtuous structures can magnify the transformative power of individuals, acting together within society.

As a theological ethicist, I see critical realist sociology as highly relevant to understanding how the church is both an agent of moral formation and a moral actor in society. Critical realism is thus a highly promising resource for Christian social ethics. Christian individuals participate in many social institutions and structures, among which the church is one. Through its organizing structures, its practices, and its "practice-laden" positions, the church is able, without voiding free will, to incorporate members into a system of purposes, symbols, roles, and actions that shape their self-understanding and behavior. Christian formation can shape agency in positive (gospel-based) directions and can structurally constrain inclinations and opportunities to think and act viciously. The Christian sacraments are good examples of this kind of incorporation and shaping. Yet membership of Christian individuals in multiple structures means that Christian teachings, practices, and rituals do not influence Christian character in direct one-to-one causation. They may compete for influence with other structural mediations of vice and virtue that shape the identities and moral choices of the same individuals or groups. In fact, through the outlooks and practices of participating individuals, ecclesial structures may eventually incorporate virtues or vices of "external" origin.

For example, members of Christian congregations also belong to political parties and civic organizations, occupying multiple and sometimes intersecting "practice-positions," leading to pluralism and tensions. Structures and their participants exist within larger cultures that can be internally diverse and contested, increasing the levels of diversity and contestation within structures themselves. As Shadle says, cultures and structures "interact and condition each other" in "complex ways." Because members of Christian churches simultaneously participate in other social structures, they are able to bring a critical imagination both to the ecclesial institution and to the surrounding culture. Yet participation in a vicious structure can distort or dilute the virtues communicated by a virtuous cultural system and the practices embodying it.

Matthew Shadle illustrates this with regard to racism. Citing Bryan Massingale, he argues that "whiteness" and "blackness" are cultural constructs that uphold a regime of socioeconomic inequality and white privilege. These structural embodiments or consequences are interdependent with racist cultural meanings and symbols. Racism will be difficult to counteract within structural systems still defined by racist cultural constructs—as can be seen when an "inclusive" Eucharistic liturgy is celebrated by a white, segregated congregation. In such a case, the "underlying set of cultural meanings" goes unchallenged until the structures and the structural participants engage not only ideationally but practically with other structures mediating alternative cultural meanings.[7] This could happen, for example, if a white church and a black church partner to meet shared communal needs in the face of a natural disaster; if a social movement such as Black Lives Matter challenges participants in segregationist ecclesial structures; or if individual participants become engaged at the personal level with a family of a different race and bring their enlarged set of meanings and expanded practices back to their "practice-positions" in the white, segregated congregation.

At the level of social ethics, structures can extend agency into a larger sphere of influence. For example, a racially inclusive church and its members are formed for political action in other structures in which they participate. Moreover, church leadership or spokespersons can introduce racial justice concerns to cultural and policy debates. More importantly, through its constitutive activities, a virtuous structure can embody and extend just practices to more people within coexisting or intersecting structures. Worldviews, individual identities, moral character, practices, cultures, and structures are all interdependent, take shape together, and together change or resist change. Moral responsibility, as both conditioned and free, must address all of these factors simultaneously. This is an important implication of critical realist sociology for theological ethics, one that helps us to better appreciate what it means to say that agency is contextual, ideas coinhere with practices, and work for justice can be effective.

In sum, a critical realist approach to freedom and agency in relation to social structures offers a more precise way for Christian ethicists and other theologians to speak of how social structures and culture influence moral agency, how structural injustice arises from inequitable restrictions and opportunities, how sin and virtue can inhere in structures and institutions and be advanced among their participants and in the wider social sphere, and how the transformation of structures can occur both by internal subversion and by the social-structural meshing of diverse practices and sets of cultural meanings.

Theological ethicists have probably always known that free will must survive despite original sin and vicious cultures or else "ethics" would be pointless. They have also believed that cultures as a whole and their members can be indicted for vices and crimes. Since at least the middle of the last century, Christian ethicists have been adamant that collective efforts toward social justice can and must be effective. Critical realism is a theory that validates all these convictions, showing in a highly specific and nuanced way just how they are existentially meaningful and reality based.

NOTES

1. Augustine, *The Spirit and the Letter*, chap. 63.
2. Thomas Aquinas, *Summa Theologiae*, II-II.Q 47.a 2.
3. See for example, Jonathan Haidt, *The Righteous Mind: Why Good People Are Divided by Politics and Religion* (New York: Random House, 2012).
4. Peter L. Berger and Thomas Luckmann, *The Social Construction of Reality: A Treatise in the Sociology of Knowledge* (Garden City, NY: Doubleday, 1966).
5. Joseph Liechty and Cecelia Clegg, *Moving beyond Sectarianism: Religion, Conflict and Reconciliation in Northern Ireland* (Dublin: Columba Press, 2001), 9.
6. Douglas V. Porpora, "Four Concepts of Social Structure," *Journal for the Theory of Social Behavior* 19, no. 2 (1989): 195.
7. Bryan Massingale, "The Systemic Erasure of the Black/Dark-Skinned Body in Catholic Ethics," in *Catholic Theological Ethics Past, Present, and Future*, ed. James F. Keenan (Maryknoll, NY: Orbis, 2011), 120.

FURTHER READING

You the reader have gotten a taste of some of the ways that critical realist sociology can provide a descriptively accurate account of how the social world affects human decision-making. The critical realist insight into social structures and culture cannot, of course, substitute for the moral analysis that is the purview of Christian ethics, but it can sharpen the way Christian ethicists understand the impact of the social world on moral agency. If this volume has been successful, you are now interested in learning more. This chapter is presented to assist you in that process.

Having been where you are now, each of the authors of this volume is vividly aware of the challenges ahead of you. The unhappy situation is that many of the primary sources in critical realism—both in sociology and philosophy—are frustratingly difficult. They tend to be quite dense, laden with disciplinary jargon, and presume the expertise of peers in those fields. In short, they are rough going for even highly intelligent newcomers from other disciplines.

Of course, the same sort of challenges would face an ethicist first taking on the medical literature necessary for biomedical ethics today or a sociologist who wanted to learn from Augustine, Aquinas, Whitehead, Lonergan, or Rahner. These are the costs of serious interdisciplinary study, something that daily life in the silos of contemporary higher education tends to discourage.

As a result, we have decided against simply presenting a list of sources here and instead propose a more prescriptive approach, suggesting a path of entry before inviting the reader to choose at will among the many alternative sources.

WHERE TO START

The most accessible texts to begin with are written by critical realist sociologists with the explicit intention of introducing others to the field. We suggest one each from leading scholars: Christian Smith, Margaret Archer, and Douglas Porpora.

Christian Smith's *What Is a Person? Rethinking Humanity, Social Life, and the Moral Good from the Person Up* (Chicago: University of Chicago Press, 2010) provides an accessible introduction to many of the themes in critical realist sociology most helpful to Christian ethics.

- Pages 25–42: a brilliant explanation of emergence and why reductionism is a mistake.
- Pages 90–98: a brief explanation of critical realism.
- Pages 119–23, 157–59, and 207–9: a helpful distinction between a strong version of the social construction of reality (it's all construction with no reliable access to reality) and a weak version (knowledge is always shaped by both reality and context). Rejecting the former, he advocates the weak version.
- Pages 317–83: social structures, where they come from, how they function, how they change.

In "Structural Conditioning and Personal Reflexivity: Sources of Market Complicity, Critique, and Change," in *Distant Markets, Distant Harms: Economic Complicity and Christian Ethics*, ed. Daniel K. Finn, 25–53 (New York: Oxford University Press, 2014), Margaret Archer, the world's foremost voice in critical realist sociology, explores how human agents and social structures exert (different) causal powers and have identifiable effects in people's lives.

Douglas Porpora, in *Reconstructing Sociology: The Critical Realist Approach* (Cambridge: Cambridge University Press, 2015), introduces the reader to critical realism and carefully distinguishes it from other, less adequate perspectives in both sociology and the philosophy of science.

DEEPER INVESTIGATION

Having gotten a better understanding of the critical realist project, you may then want to dig deeper in both critical realist sociology and in the philosophy of science that undergirds it. Which of these sources you turn to will, of course, depend on your interests.

Sociology

Margaret Archer, *Realist Social Theory: The Morphogenetic Approach* (Cambridge: Cambridge University Press, 1995).

Margaret Archer, *Structure, Agency and the Internal Conversation* (Cambridge: Cambridge University Press, 2003).

Margaret Archer, *Culture and Agency: The Place of Culture and Social Theory*, rev. ed. (Cambridge: Cambridge University Press, 1996).

Dave Elder-Vass, *The Causal Power of Social Structures: Emergence, Structure and Agency* (Cambridge: Cambridge University Press, 2010).
Dave Elder-Vass, *The Reality of Social Construction* (Cambridge: Cambridge University Press, 2012).

Philosophy of Science

Roy Bhaskar, *A Realist Theory of Science*, 2nd ed. (London: Verso, 2008). (This is the "bible" of critical realist philosophy of science.)
A more accessible treatment of Bhaskar's realist approach appears in Peter T. Manicas, *A Realist Philosophy of Science: Explanation and Understanding* (Cambridge: Cambridge University Press, 2006).
Roy Bhaskar, *The Possibility of Naturalism: A Philosophical Critique of the Contemporary Human Sciences*, 3rd ed. (London: Routledge, 1998).

CONCLUSION

The chapters of this primer, and even the readings listed above, provide only a short introduction to critical realism, a large and growing field of intellectual inquiry. As Yale sociologist Philip S. Gorski put it, "It has a journal, a book series, an association, an annual meeting and, in short, all the usual trappings of an intellectual movement."[1] Thus, the literature is immense and exhibits the diversity of a young and lively movement. It is unlikely that anyone in Christian ethics will become "an expert" in critical realism.

We point out these realities here not to discourage the reader with a daunting challenge of taking on an impossible task but simply to acknowledge the riches that are available. The insights of critical realist sociology open up a host of potential research opportunities for scholars in Christian ethics and in theology more broadly, opportunities to apply a more precise and adequate grasp of the social world to illuminate many traditional theological questions. As David Cloutier puts it in chapter 1, critical realism

> can improve the way ecclesiology understands the internal dynamics of a church, the way patristics explains the influence of Roman authorities on the Fathers, the way liturgical theology understands the formative dimension of weekly worship, the way biblical studies interpret the mutual influences of different literary traditions, the way fundamental moral theology explains the influence of society on the virtue of individuals, the way pastoral theology describes the relation between pastor and lay ministers, the way bioethicists understand the relation of doctor and patient in a health crisis, and more.

Critical realism provides sociological, not theological, insight. But its more adequate understanding of the social world promises to deepen theological understanding and, ultimately, to assist in the announcement of the good news of the Gospel in a world in such deep need of it.

NOTES

1. Philip S. Gorski, "What Is Critical Realism? And Why Should You Care?," *Contemporary Sociology* 42, no. 5 (2013): 658.

INDEX

ABOUT THE
CONTRIBUTORS

DAVID CLOUTIER is an associate professor of moral theology at Catholic University of America in Washington, DC. A graduate of Carleton College and Duke University, he is the author of *The Vice of Luxury: Economic Excess in a Consumer Age* (Georgetown) and *Walking God's Earth: The Environment and Catholic Theology* (Liturgical). His current work includes a grant from the Happiness and Well-Being Project at Saint Louis University, supporting collaborative work with a psychologist to integrate virtue ethics with empirical models in psychology. He writes frequently for *Commonweal* magazine and is the editor of the academic group blog catholicmoraltheology.com.

DANIEL J. DALY is an associate professor of moral theology at Boston College, School of Theology and Ministry. He received his doctorate in theological ethics from Boston College in 2008. He has served as a clinical medical ethicist at the hospital level and serves on the Theologian/Ethicist Committee of the Catholic Health Association. His work has been published in *Angelicum, Christian Bioethics, Heythrop Journal,* and *New Blackfriars.*

DANIEL K. FINN is a professor of theology and the Clemens Professor of Economics at the College of St. Benedict and St. John's University. He is a former president of the Catholic Theological Society of America, the Society of Christian Ethics, and the Association for Social Economics. His books include *Consumer Ethics in a Global Economy: How Buying Here Causes Injustice There* (Georgetown), *Christian Economic Ethics: History and Implications* (Fortress), and *The Moral Ecology of Markets: A Framework for Assessing Justice in Economic Life* (Cambridge). He is the director of the True Wealth of Nations research project at the Institute for Advanced Catholic Studies in Los Angeles.

THEODORA HAWKSLEY is a British Catholic theologian specializing in peacebuilding and Catholic social teaching. She is a contributing editor and author for *Peacebuilding and the Arts* (Palgrave Macmillan, 2019), edited by Hal Culbertson, Theodora Hawksley, Jolyon Mitchell, and Giselle Vincett, and a contributing author to the forthcoming *Wiley Blackwell Companion to Religion and Peace*. Her book, *What Makes for Peace: Peacebuilding and Catholic Social Teaching*, is forthcoming from the University of Notre Dame Press.

MATTHEW A. SHADLE is an associate professor of theology and religious studies at Marymount University in Arlington, Virginia. His research focuses on the role of identity and imagination in theological and ethical reflection on contentious social issues, and it explores the intersection of theology and social theory. He has published *The Origins of War: A Catholic Perspective* (Georgetown) and *Interrupting Capitalism: Catholic Social Thought and the Economy* (Oxford). His work has been published in several scholarly journals, such as the *Journal of the Society of Christian Ethics, Horizons, Political Theology*, and the *Journal of Catholic Social Thought*. He has presented at the US Army Command and General Staff College in Ft. Leavenworth, Kansas, and represents the United States Conference of Catholic Bishops at the National Council of Churches' Faith and Order Convening Table.